THE
ESCAPE
FACTORY

July 20, 1992

To Mr. Elwyn Blacker
With Sincere
Best Wishes —

Lloyd R. Shoemaker

POW cage at "P.O. Box 1142." *(National Archives)*

THE
ESCAPE
FACTORY

The Story of MIS-X

—————×———×———×———×—————

LLOYD R. SHOEMAKER

ST. MARTIN'S PRESS
NEW YORK

Production Editor: Mark H. Berkowitz
Copy Editor: Linda Venator
Designer: Jaye Zimet

Library of Congress Cataloging-in-Publication Data

Shoemaker, Lloyd R.
    The escape factory.
        p.   cm.
    ISBN 0-312-03826-7
    1. World War, 1939–1945—Secret service—United States.   2. World
War, 1939–1945—Prisoners and prisons.   3. Escapes—History—20th
century.   I. Title.
D810.S7S46   1990   940.54'8673—dc20   89-24174

First Edition

10   9   8   7   6   5   4   3   2   1

This book is dedicated to the thousands of American prisoners of war who continued their fight on the barbed-wire Front, and to the handful of men who helped them win it.

Prisoner of War! That is the least unfortunate kind of prisoner to be, but it is nevertheless a melancholy state. You are in the power of your enemy. You owe your life to his humanity, and your daily bread to his compassion. You must obey his orders, go where he tells you, stay where you are bid, await his pleasure, possess your soul in patience.

—WINSTON S. CHURCHILL

CONTENTS

FOREWORD

THIS BOOK DEALS WITH a secret aspect of the war against the Axis powers that has hitherto received little notice in the United States, and deals with it from a fully informed insider's angle of sight. Mr. Shoemaker rose only to the rank of corporal; that did not keep him from exercising an influence on the course of the war, which the passage of time and his own careful research now allow him to reveal.

As far back as the autumn of 1939, the future field marshal, Sir Gerald W. R. Templer, then in charge of security with the British Expeditionary Force in France, put to the British War Office the notion that it would be well to have some secret means of remaining in touch with prisoners in enemy hands. From Templer's proposal grew MI-9, the British service that trained the armed forces in how to behave if captured and, far more secretly, in how to send messages out of prison camps, how to escape from them, or (better still) how to evade capture altogether.

Templer's friend Norman Crockatt, in charge of MI-9, was aware that he came under the watchful eye of

Claude Dansey, the éminence grise of the still more secret MI-6; but he had a mind of his own, strong empathy with prisoners of war, and a steady eye on the real needs of the Anglo-American alliance. As soon as the United States entered the war, Crockatt laid all his secrets open to the American intelligence staffs, who set up within the military intelligence directorate a little branch, MIS-X, that did MI-9's work for the American armed forces.

Lloyd Shoemaker was a craftsman in MIS-X who helped to secure such things as cameras, silk maps, and radio sets and to conceal them in innocent objects— baseball bats, shaving brushes, shoe brushes, packs of cards or of cigarettes—and to smuggle them into prisoner of war camps. He testifies to the extreme discretion in which all this work was veiled, in a society that prided itself on being entirely open. At the end of the war, in the autumn of 1945, MIS-X's records were destroyed, as were most of the remaining artifacts, on orders from high authority. This has not prevented him from piecing together this remarkable addition to history.

This book at once enhances our understanding of how the war was won and adds several splendid new pages to the world's collection of stories about how tyranny can be outfaced. Shoemaker's accounts, for example, of how to smuggle parcels past the sharp nose of a Gestapo inspector show that the best way of doing so was by the time-honored methods of the best con men: beautiful manners, a deft distraction of the victim's attention at the critical moment, and split-second timing of the sleight of hand.

He writes, clearly and modestly, from his own knowledge, from what old men remember, and from what can be quarried from the archives, where a lot more survived than authority had intended. Many of the tales he tells are stranger than fiction; that does not make them any less authentic.

London, England   M. R. D. FOOT

PREFACE

DURING WORLD WAR II, a secret unit was created within the military structure of the War Department. Known only by the initials MIS-X, this unit was to be responsible for initiating and overseeing all escape and evasion efforts of the United States. So covert was it that the Congress of the United States and the military leadership knew nothing of its existence.

Today virtually no records or principals of this agency have survived to tell its story. President Franklin Delano Roosevelt; Henry L. Stimson, secretary of war; Major General George V. Strong, assistant chief of staff G-2; General Carl Spaatz, U.S. Air Corps; Brigadier Norman Crockatt, British MI-9; Colonel Catesby ap Jones, POW Branch; Colonel Russell Sweet, commanding officer, MIS-Y; and Colonel J. Edward Johnston, commanding officer, MIS-X—all are dead.

While time and age have obscured their recollections, Colonel Robley E. Winfrey, commanding officer, technical and codes sections; Major Leo H. Crosson, technical section; Sergeant Carl Peterson and Master Sergeant Silvio A. Bedini; and the author (also a participant) managed to piece together a factual outline of this unique unit and to obtain objects and photographs thought to be lost or destroyed. Some of the pictures located by the author were found to have been made inside POW camps in Germany, using cameras and film smuggled in by MIS-X, and a sampling is included in this book.

THE ESCAPE FACTORY

1

———✗————✗———

AT WAR

IN THE SUMMER OF 1945, five days after Japan capitulated and World War II ended, the U.S. assistant chief of staff G-2, Major General George V. Strong, issued an order to burn all records, files, and artifacts of an ultrasecret government agency that had been covertly located within U.S. borders and known only by the code name MIS-X. Immediately the buildings that housed this agency were demolished, the fences surrounding it were torn down, the grounds on which it had stood were planted over with trees, and all military personnel involved were summarily discharged.

By summer's end virtually all physical and written evidence of MIS-X had been effectively obliterated. The agency that for the past three years had maintained covert radio and letter-code communication with the ninety-five thousand U.S. POWs in Europe and had been responsible for most American POW escape and evasion activities was now itself concealed. Neither the Military General Staff of the United States nor the chief of the Air Force Intelligence Training Command, Colonel E. W. Ridings, could locate enough information about MIS-

X just three years after World War II to reactivate a similar escape and evasion agency in preparation for the impending Korean War. As a top secret communique by Ridings stated at the time, "The whole activity [of MIS-X] was conducted with the greatest secrecy. Over-all operational control was in the hands of a few officers in Washington. Most of these officers were not regular officers. Consequently, almost no knowledge of [MIS-X's] activity exists in the Regular Service."[1] The agency that had thrived on disguise and illusion had become thoroughly invisible.

To tell its story, then, we must first weave together the severed threads of its past. . . .

On December 7, 1941, Japan bombed Pearl Harbor, and the United States became a nation offended and mobilized. Suddenly, overnight, thousands of fervent young men lined up angrily before recruiting stations, clamoring to revenge the smoking American hulks now laying violated in Hawaii's waters. Only twenty-four hours earlier, they had been unmoved by Nazi Germany's violations of European sovereignty.

But the United States had no wartime organization or machinery to give substance or support to its fury. Its only intelligence agency was the Military Intelligence Division, a peacetime attaché network whose limited complement of approximately two hundred officers was based exclusively in foreign embassies, restricted to acquiring whatever secrets it could through "polite eavesdropping."

With feverish energy, therefore, the Military Intelligence Service was quickly organized to handle the now urgent need for a wartime American intelligence operation. It rapidly acquired a dizzying array of departments and subdepartments and a staff numbering in the hundreds.

Buried deep within this burgeoning complex, and

critical to the story of MIS-X, was a department in-
nocuously labeled Prisoner of War Branch. Responsible
for maintaining files on America POWs, the Prisoner of
War Branch attracted little attention, appearing to be
but another bureaucratic necessity of a nation at war.
Under its jurisdiction, however, was a single subdepartment whose formal name was Military Intelligence Service-Y, or MIS-Y. MIS-Y was not to be another routine
record-keeping department. Instead, it was to oversee a
limited-capacity interrogation camp on American soil
where enemy POWs suspected of knowing vital information could be clandestinely brought from Europe and
held for ten to twenty days of intensive intelligence questioning.[2]

Appointed to command the Pentagon's office for
MIS-Y was a successful Rhode Island businessman and
real estate developer in his mid-fifties by the name of
Colonel Russell H. Sweet. Though not a professional
soldier, Sweet's business and organizational skills had
provided him with the instincts of a seasoned officer and
the determination to read all obstacles as challenges.
Dignified and articulate, he was capable of putting everyone at ease who came before him. When Sweet drew up
his table of organization for MIS-Y, it was quickly and
enthusiastically approved by the commander of the Prisoner of War Branch, Sweet's superior, Colonel Catesby
ap Jones.

A professional soldier from a wealthy and distin-
guished Virginia family involved in the railroad, banking, and cotton industries, Catesby ap Jones was the
grandson of the commander of the fabled Civil War iron-
clad *Virginia* (originally the frigate *Merrimack*). Beginning his own military career as a sergeant under General
"Black Jack" Pershing along the Mexican border in
1916, Jones received his commission as a second lieutenant when the United States entered World War I and in
1918 sailed for France with the American Expeditionary

Force (AEF). In 1941 he was in his early sixties and serving out his military career in the Virginia National Guard when he was asked to head the Prisoner of War Branch.

Possessed of a long-standing military pride, Jones practiced a methodicalness that would permit nothing to be overlooked, considering any oversight to be a potential personal blemish or costly vulnerability. When he learned of his nomination to head the Prisoner of War Branch, he accepted the position with an eye toward it representing the fulfillment of his personal military achievements.

Upon assuming command, Jones assigned Sweet to begin recruiting linguistic interrogators and turned his own attention to obtaining a location he had been considering for the POW camp.

Twenty miles south of Washington, D.C., high on the west bank of the Potomac River, lay eighty acres of land that had been a Civil War and World War I military post. Originally a part of George Washington's Mount Vernon estate, all that remained of this land's rich past were a World War I coast artillery gun emplacement bunker, an officers' quarters that served as the groundskeeper's residence, and the name Fort Hunt. Unoccupied and surrounded on all sides by dense rows of trees, it was currently being used by the citizens of nearby Alexandria, Virginia, as a picnic area and lovers' roost.

Jones knew, however, that Fort Hunt would make an ideal site for a POW and interrogation camp, as its proximity to Washington would allow sensitive information to be transmitted quickly to the General Staff. Arranging a meeting with the Interior Department, to whom the land had reverted, Jones returned with a lease to the fort for the duration of the war plus one year.[3]

By April 1942—under Sweet's supervision and with the aid of his newly appointed post commander and chief interrogator, Colonel John Walker—the recently quiet site of Fort Hunt, Virginia, had returned to its former military cast. The quarters, supply, mess, and administration buildings had been erected, construction of a POW pen was completed, and a full complement of interrogators and MP guard personnel was on hand. America's only interrogation camp was ready for operation.

Every morning the bugle sounded reveille as the cannon fired at 0600 hours for the four hundred soldiers billeted at the fort, and every evening it sounded retreat at 1700 hours, to lower the flag and end the day.

Secrecy from the community was not and could not be a concern, as daily reveille and retreat rippled across the countryside, and a procession of olive green, windowless buses rolled through Alexandria's streets, accompanied by Jeeps occupied by military policemen armed with shotguns. The city of Alexandria believed, however, that Fort Hunt was strictly a POW camp. It did not know that it was an information-gathering center, similar to the German *Dulagen* in Europe, where POWs thought to know something of importance were interned. It did not know that "cooperative" German POWs were being flown from England in darkened airplanes, picked up in the windowless buses that moved mysteriously through the town, and brought to Fort Hunt to be "milked" for information.[4] Not even the city or county police or fire departments knew of this. Not even later, when German POWs sat in the city's restaurants and theaters, dressed in their country's uniforms and surrounded by military police—their lives considered to be too much at risk for them to be returned to Germany—would the people of Alexandria know what was truly going on.

And neither the citizens of Alexandria nor the members of Congress would ever know that inside Fort Hunt was to be yet another department of the Military Intelligence Service known as MIS-X, where some of the most covert and sensitive activities of the war would be carried out. Even Colonel Walker, commanding officer of the fort, though of necessity aware that MIS-X was based on his post, would never have any direct knowledge of what this unit was all about.

And neither would anyone else in the United States in the early part of 1942—for the remaining events leading toward MIS-X's existence would take place abroad.

2

---X---X---

THE BARBED-WIRE
FRONT

In February 1942, U.S. Major General Carl Spaatz arrived in London to begin preliminary arrangements for the movement of his Army Eighth Air Force command to England. In the course of his briefings on the status of the war and British Intelligence operations, Spaatz met with Brigadier Norman Crockatt, chief of Britain's Prisoner of War Branch, who acquainted him with the unusual activities of a department under Crockatt's command known as Military Intelligence-9 (MI-9).

Created at the end of 1939, MI-9 had come into being amid anxious and emotional circumstances: fifty thousand British soldiers fighting the rear-guard action at the evacuation of Dunkirk became prisoners of war in 1940. Determined to rescue these men, the British were inspired by the fact that, in World War I, 107,000 of their 2.5 million POWs had escaped from German prison camps without having received any special assistance whatsoever.[1]

In this war, however, they knew times and conditions had dramatically changed: Hitler had decreed that all POW camps be located in eastern Europe, one thousand miles from the English Channel; and advances in radio, telephone, and methods of transportation were profoundly and irreversibly altering military as well as civilian lives. POWs who attempted to escape would be required to travel greater distances to reach safety—and radio and telephone alerts, as well as automobile and motorcycle search parties, could travel these same distances faster.

But the greatest impediment to POWs in this war was the transformation of Germany to a police state: every movement of every person was subject to scrutiny. Strangers would not be ignored, could not be inconspicuously lost in a crowd.

A successful escape and evasion agency, therefore, had to have at its disposal the most current information available, from every front. Consequently, MI-9 was created as an intraservice department within the Prisoner of War Branch, staffed by the British army, navy, and air force. It was charged with the responsibility of developing sophisticated escape devices and letter codes to assist British servicemen in escape and evasion activities.

By the time Spaatz sat down with Crockatt in the winter of 1942, MI-9 had established fictitious humanitarian organizations that were surreptitiously delivering to POWs escape aids hidden in game boards, soap, shaving brushes, and razors. RAF servicemen were being routinely supplied with a compass concealed somewhere in their clothing, smoking materials, or pen and pencil clips, as well as maps of areas over which they would be flying. Passport photos in waterproof casings were being sewn into uniforms along with extraordinarily sharp, hardened gigili saws to be used for cutting through metal. Escape kits containing dry food, money (French, Belgian, English, and Dutch gold and paper), safety pins, needle and thread, and matches were standard equipment for every British flier. Forged German travel and work permits and forged French discharge papers allowed downed British airmen to move across Europe without arousing German suspicion, posing as French servicemen whom the Germans, having dissolved the French army, were now using as craftsmen and technicians in the German war industry.

Daily communication with POWs had already been established through sophisticated secret letter codes and training programs, and roughly 750 POWs had already been assisted in their escape efforts through organized escape committees in the POW camps.

"As an example," said Crockatt, "we just helped two Dutch officers escape from Colditz, a stone castle located on a high bluff twenty miles southeast of Leipzig that the Germans considered escape-proof. Only POWs who have already attempted escapes from other camps or whom the Germans considered troublesome or noteworthy are sent there. We got these officers to Switzerland, where they then wrote a coded letter back to Colditz, inform the remaining POWs that their escape was successful and telling them of their escape route and circumstances. Thirty days later we picked them up and brought them here to MI-9, where they began loading chessboards and chess pieces with files and German bank notes and maps."

Spaatz listened to Crockatt with growing awe. Perhaps the most unique and, to Spaatz, incredible aspect of MI-9 was that it was actively to inspire air crews and commandos with the will to escape. MI-9 was to create a never-before-realized military unit—the POW—and with it challenge Hitler at his own game.

As POW camps were, under Hitler's orders, located in remote corners of Germany's occupied territories, the British ingeniously reasoned that if there could be a constant threat of escapees and evaders roaming the countryside deep within Germany's lines, Hitler would have to reserve large numbers of his military personnel and civilian police for apprehension of this footloose enemy manpower. Front-line forces would thus be significantly reduced, and German morale would be adversely affected.

So stunned was Spaatz by the successes and audacity of MI-9 as he listened to Crockatt that he formally petitioned British intelligence authorities to come to the United States and repeat this briefing to the American General Staff in Washington. Then, convinced that the United States would enthusiastically create a similar agency within its own military department, he took it upon himself to request permission from MI-9 to attach an American officer to MI-9's staff to learn everything there was to know about escape and evasion devices and activities.

Sitting idly on Spaatz's staff at this time was a forty-two-year-old commissioned officer by the name of Robley E. Winfrey. A former professor of civil engineering at Iowa State University, Winfrey had applied for direct commission at the outbreak of World War II, which he was granted in the grade of captain. He was then assigned to the air force to oversee airfield construction, which brought him under Spaatz's command.

Sailing for London in early February 1942 to assist Spaatz in setting up a base in England, Winfrey and other staff members were but two days out of port when their ship was torpedoed and they had to be rescued at sea. Returning to Baltimore, Winfrey boarded another ship two days later, which was once again, after two days at sea, torpedoed. Rescued once more, the captain, amazingly undaunted, boarded yet another ship and sailed uneventfully, finally arriving in England in mid-February.[2]

But he soon found himself bored and restless: England had no need at this time for new airfields. Daily he begged an aide of Spaatz's to find him something of consequence to do. When the aide heard of the special assignment Spaatz was planning for MI-9, therefore, he asked Winfrey if he wanted to be recommended for the position. Winfrey unhesitatingly accepted, though he was totally unaware of what the job entailed.

Shortly thereafter, Winfrey received orders to report to Brigadier Crockatt at the British Prisoner of War Branch in room 527 of the Victoria Hotel in London. When he met Crockatt and heard what his assignment involved, Winfrey recalls being "thunderstruck at the anticipation of the idea; elated to have an assignment, and to participate in such shenanigans upon a foreign government."[3]

Spaatz, meanwhile, had completed a month of extensive briefings and was ready to return to the United States and begin the movement of his command to England. Before he left, however, he was determined to convince the U.S. General Staff to learn about this amazing British agency by the name of MI-9 that was successfully aiding and supplying English POWs behind German lines. As a result of his insistent promptings, British Air Vice-Marshall Charles Medhurst left England for the United States in March 1942 to acquaint Chief of Staff General George C. Marshall and Secretary of War Henry L. Stimson with MI-9.[4]

Stimson was not impressed. It was inconceivable, he thought, that such an agency could succeed. It was, by his reasoning, an idea more appropriate to the art of science fiction than the science of military strategy.

Spaatz, however, was not to be deterred, and by June 1942, when he returned to England to enter the war with his U.S. Army Eighth Air Force, he had secured Stimson's consent. England's indisputable success with MI-9 and the additional urging of General Marshall and Major General George V. Strong had persuaded Stimson of the feasibility of a U.S. escape and evasion agency.

But the powers that be move slowly, and it was not until October 1942 that Stimson advised Prisoner of War Branch commander Catesby ap Jones that a second department would now be established at Fort Hunt under his command, to be called MIS-X. Consisting of five subsections—interrogation, correspondence, POW locations, training and briefing, and technical—this new department was given the following missions:

    a. Indoctrinate Air Force [A-2 and ground force S-2] intelligence officers who will in turn instruct air crews in the various Theaters of Operation on evasion of capture when forced down or captured in enemy territory.

    b. Instructions on escape—including the instilling of escape psychology in combat airmen and communicating plans for escape to American prisoners of war by means of codes.

    c. Instruction in proper conduct after capture and to inform intelligence officers of the rights of prisoners of war under international law.

    d. To secure military information from American or Allied escaped prisoners on their return to Allied territory.

    e. To obtain by means of codes from prisoners of war still in captivity information concerning locations of prisoners, conditions of imprisonment, opportunities for escape, reasons for failure in attempts to escape, and other pertinent intelligence.

    f. To assist in the preparation and distribution of escape kits, and emergency kits containing maps, money, and other necessities to be furnished air crews on missions and to incorporate new ideas and improvements in such equipment.

    g. Plan and carry on correspondence with prisoners of war by means of codes which will be taught to key personnel of this organization.

h. To maintain close liaison with the British MI-9 branch, which is conducting similar operations.[5]

Unlike MIS-Y, however, MIS-X was to be an ultra-secret agency whose finances and activities were to be scrupulously concealed even from government and military inquiry. Stimson next directed, therefore, "that necessary funds for execution of the functions of this section be provided from sources under the control of the Secretary of War or from such other sources, other than routine channels, as may be made available."[6] He then released $25,000 from his department's war appropriations to put MIS-X in motion.

The moment he learned that MIS-X would be a second subdepartment of his Prisoner of War Branch, Catesby ap Jones knew that Fort Hunt would be the ideal site for its technical and correspondence operations. MIS-Y could easily house and conceal the small cadre of officers, technicians, and correspondents needed to staff MIS-X as well as supply their normal military requirements. Though MIS-X would fall under a separate command, its personnel could easily be billeted with MIS-Y personnel, eat in the same mess hall, and have its payroll and supplies handled by the post administrative staff. And the already on-site military police security force would ensure MIS-X's secrecy. MIS-Y personnel, however, were to have no knowledge of MIS-X activities, and MIS-X was to have no garrison duties beyond its own internal needs for high security.

Jones next appointed Colonel J. Edward Johnston to be the Pentagon's commanding officer for MIS-X. A keen businessman who had served as a senior executive in the R. J. Reynolds Tobacco Company and had amassed a fortune in the stock market by cashing in a few weeks before the crash of 1929, Johnston, upon receiving his appointment, flew to London for two weeks to meet with Brigadier Crockatt and Lieutenant Colonel W. Stull Holt, an officer whom Spaatz had assigned to MI-9 as the American military liaison.[7]

At the same time, Winfrey was returning to the United States from London after completing five months of intensive training in escape and evasion procedures under the supervision of Brigadier Crockatt. Upon arriving in the States, he was detached to Fort Hunt, Virginia, where he was appointed on-site commander for MIS-X.[8]

It was now October 1942, just under a year since World War II had begun, and the paths leading toward the birth of MIS-X had finally converged.

Briefers had to be trained and moved into the field quickly.

And they were.

Second Lieutenant Harry L. Osterweis, one of the first five officers of the correspondence section, was trained as a briefer. Barely in MIS-X for a month, he was transferred to London, where he worked with Sir William Stephenson (INTREPID) in setting up the censoring station in Bermuda. Soon thereafter he was shifted to North Africa and then almost immediately sent to the South Pacific theater, where he served in General Douglas MacArthur's Allied Intelligence Bureau until V-J Day, returning home a Lieutenant Colonel.[1]

The optimism and bravado of many of the first U.S. servicemen often counteracted Winfrey's efforts. Overconfident pilots frequently left their E&E kits and materials behind in their barracks, and many who were shot down early in the war were consequently taken prisoner and remained helplessly confined in POW camps. As stories of POW camp mistreatment spread, however, these lapses were minimized, and countless servicemen trapped behind enemy lines were able to avoid capture and make their way back to Allied bases.

Many of those who were captured carried with them critical information that made them invaluable links in MIS-X's vital communication network. While training air and ground forces in E&E tactics and procedures, some of the briefers were additionally secretly selecting two men from each squadron and battalion and teaching them the letter codes used in the Creamery. Each trained code user (CU) was given a code name and instructed that, if captured, he was to advise his camp's Allied commanding officer that he was a code user and possessed the means of maintaining contact with the U.S. War Department. Using the prevailing U.S. mail system, the code user would write a conventional letter to a family member and conceal within it a coded message. The CU had no idea how or by whom that coded message would be intercepted, only that somehow it would reach the proper authorities in the U.S. government.

Knowledge of these codes was the only secret MIS-X information to which the briefers were ever privy, and so guarded was this information that not even every briefer was taught the codes by Winfrey and Winterbottom—only those who were considered most trustworthy and competent.

By war's end, however, this system had become so efficient that MIS-X briefers had taught 7,724 military personnel the letter codes, and MIS-X was able to maintain constant communication with American POWs in virtually every German POW camp.[2] And so well selected were these code users that not one ever broke security. Indeed, they never even knew each other's names. Not until 1986, at a Stalag Luft III reunion in Seattle, Washington, was the identity of a single World War II CU ever revealed—forty-one years after the war had ended!

Amazingly, MIS-X personnel had been able to maintain greater secrecy than those associated with the atomic bomb project. Sustaining this secrecy and making it work, however, required that Winfrey seek the assistance of an additional department within the U.S. government.

In World War II, the Allied nations developed the first efficient global censorship organization. Each nation supervised its own operation, but cooperation was so effective that there were few delays in communication.

In the United States, the office of censorship was established under the War Powers Act on December 18, 1941. Forty-eight hours later, Byron Price, executive news editor for the Associated Press, was selected by President Roosevelt to be the director of censorship, a title that additionally permitted him to take immediate control of the censoring activities that were already under way on a limited basis within the army and navy.

Located on the fifteenth floor of 90 Church Street in New York, the censoring department's sorting office oversaw all mail to or from POWs in Europe and was headed by Frederick W. Siegel, a retired postal supervisor commissioned as colonel. Letters to POWs in Europe were identified by the camp address on the envelope, and letters from POWs were identified by the red or purple German postmark with the accompanying swastika.[3]

Winfrey obtained a dozen censor's stamps and arranged to have a list of the names and addresses of all known POWs who were code users posted in each of the twenty-four cubicles at 90 Church Street, where female sorters picked through hundreds of thousands of letters daily. Should the name of a CU appear, the sorter was to pass the envelope on to her supervisor, who would then direct it to Siegel. It would then be put in a sealed pouch placed aboard a daily military air shuttle to Bolling Air Force Base, Maryland, via courier plane. An MIS-X officer then picked up the bags and brought them to 1142. The code users who decoded the signals were all stationed in one room in the Creamery, seated at a table that was twenty-two feet long. Fourteen cryptoanalysts worked at this table, seven on each side, with a wooden partition separating them to ensure privacy. In addition to decoding incoming mail, each of the code users in the Creamery wrote letters to from ten to twenty POW CUs, pretending to be girlfriends, wives, fathers, siblings, or just friends. They each had their own distinct stationery to avoid arousing the suspicion of the German censors.

When the mailbags arrived in the Creamery, the chief cryptoanalyst or chief briefer would unlock the bags and separate the coded letters from the rest of the POW mail. Each "hot" letter was then steamed open and the message decoded. Then the letter was resealed and returned to the mailbags, which were relocked; one to two hours after receipt, the bags were sent to the post office in Alexandria, where an informed supervisor slipped the letters back into the postal system for normal delivery. All coded letters were immediately decoded and directed to Winfrey with a copy going to the Pentagon via daily courier.

The friends, lovers, wives, and families who were the recipients of these coded letters had no idea that the letters they were receiving from a POW had been opened or that the text contained a secret message. To them, the letters looked to be ordinary mail from a loved one held behind barbed wire.

In October 1942, however, though the censoring system was in effect and operating, MIS-X had few secrets and the United States had no letter code of its own. The technical section of MIS-X was not even in existence—there was not even a building to house it. That was now to come.

When Colonel Catesby ap Jones ordered the renovation of the groundskeeper's house for the MIS-X correspondence section, he also ordered that a building be constructed nearby for the technical section. Given the code name "the Warehouse," it was to be located across the street from the Creamery and would house the mechanical shop, the printing press, the parcel room, the briefing room, and Winfrey's official administrative office.

Construction was completed in December 1942, and Winfrey—leaving Captain John Starr and the chief briefer, Captain Creighton Churchill, in the Creamery to develop proficiency in the letter codes and train new briefers—moved his permanent headquarters into the fifteen-by-fifteen-foot room that he would now share with two clerk typists for the remainder of the war. It was the only room in the Warehouse that had heat.

Designed in keeping with the wood frame structures commonly used by the military during World War II, the Warehouse comprised a center section flanked by two wings measuring seventy-five by twenty-five feet each. A single entry that led into the center section provided the only access into the building and Winfrey's office.

To the left of the center section, an alarm-fitted security door guarded the large technicians' wing, where supplies would be received and the secret escape and evasion materials would be designed, built, and shipped. At the far end of this wing, away from the entry door, the floor was reinforced to support the weight of a printing press, and eight-foot-high supply shelves stood nearby against the back wall. Several feet forward from where the press would be was another storage shelf in the center of the floor, and in front of it, a sixteen-foot-long smooth-topped counter that would be used as a packaging table.

Built off the rear of this wing was a smaller room measuring twenty-five by fifty feet. Named "the Shop" because it was where the E&E materials would be developed, it contained a table that ran the fifty-foot length of one wall, six freestanding work stations, and a seventh table in the back corner for counting gold and paper currency.

Across the way from the Shop were solid-core double doors fitted with security locks that opened onto the technical wing's loading dock. A cupboard nearby held the mailbags and mailbag locks used for delivering parcels to the post office.

So sensitive were the activities of the Warehouse in general, and this one wing in particular, that once the building was occupied it was never permitted to be uninhabited. Toward the front of this technical wing, not far from the Shop, was a ten-foot-square cubicle containing two bunk beds for the men whose MIS-X responsibilities would additionally include living in the building as security guards for the length of their service. Next to this cubicle were a shower and bathroom.

In the opposite wing of the Warehouse, also seventy-five feet long and twenty-five feet wide and protected by a security door, was the briefing room. It contained only chairs and, at the far end, a blackboard.

When Winfrey anxiously moved MIS-X's field headquarters into the Warehouse, the large technical wing was empty and quiet. It would be some months before the technicians would arrive and production of escape and evasion materials could begin. In the meantime Winfrey continued training his briefers and, with the $25,000 that Stimson had allocated, began purchasing the machinery and equipment that his technicians would eventually use.

Winfrey's singlehanded productivity and efficiency were not going unnoticed, and by New Year's Day, 1943, he was promoted to the rank of major. But as appreciative as he was of the recognition, it was not until late February that he received what he really wanted: three officers and nine technicians arrived at 1142 to begin work in the technical section.

Eagerly, Winfrey brought his crew into the technical wing of the Warehouse, sat them on the packing counter at the end of the room (there were no chairs), and began briefing them on the overall mission of MIS-X. None of them had been informed of the covert nature or activities of their new assignment. As Spaatz had over a year before, they listened, stunned and excited, as Winfrey told them of MI-9 and MIS-X.

"Will it really work?" asked Sergeant William Harris, who was to be in charge of the Shop's crew.

"It has for the British over the last two and a half years," Winfrey answered.

Bringing the briefing to a close, Winfrey directed the technicians to begin setting up the woodworking machinery and electrical equipment. Giving the three officers cash, he instructed them to go into town and buy shoe brushes, shaving brushes, Ping-Pong sets, and layered paper products such as checkerboards, Monopoly games, and talcum powder in waxed paper cones to begin testing materials and methods for loading.

But steaming open the layered sections of the game boards proved to be troublesome, as the different papers and glues exhibited different reactions to the steam. Some papers accepted the moisture and dried without a trace; others crumbled into mush. Some glues dissolved easily, allowing the papers to separate; others remained impervious to moisture.

Fires flared up, making the worktables extremely hazardous, with their open-flame Bunsen burners, electric steamers, and lacquer solvents. A no-smoking policy was therefore put into effect and rigidly enforced, and extra fire extinguishers were mounted on the premises. All personnel were then required to attend a special four-hour training lecture and demonstration on fire fighting at the post fire department located at nearby Fort Belvoir.

England's MI-9 had experienced few of these difficulties, as British manufacturing processes and materials differed from those used in the United States and responded more favorably to loading techniques. MIS-X, however, could not avail itself of British supplies—if American POWs were ever caught receiving parcels shipped from the United States containing products manufactured in England, the E&E efforts of both nations would be jeopardized.

In time, the U.S. Army Chemical Corps would solve some of these problems, and more selective purchasing would solve others: different manufacturers of the same games, it was eventually discovered, used different grades of papers and glues, and those that were most suitable would become the only ones used. For now, though, Winfrey could do nothing but encourage his skilled technicians to continue their painstaking experiments, racing to keep up with America's increasing involvement in the war.

And in the meantime there still remained the task of perfecting packaging procedures for getting parcels into POW camps.

Colonel J. Edward Johnston,
Commanding Officer, MIS-X. *(Mrs. Ed Thomas)*

POW transport van, MIS-Y, known as "P.O. Box 1142,
Alexandria, Virginia." *(National Archives)*

Colonel Robley E. Winfrey,
Commanding Officer,
Technical and Codes
Section, MIS-X. *(Author's
collection)*

The Warehouse housed the
Technical Section.
(Silvio A. Bedini)

The Creamery housed the Correspondence and Codes
Section of MIS-X. *(Author's collection)*

4

———✗———✗———

UNCLE SAM'S
GENERAL MERC

WITH HIS CREWS occupied with technical problems, Winfrey turned his attention to the next phase of MIS-X's organizational development. He had the letter codes for communicating with POWs, and his technicians were preparing the vehicles for concealing materials to be used in escapes—but if the entire enterprise was to work, he needed a means for delivering parcels into the camps. By common agreement, Red Cross packages would not be exploited and used to conceal escape and evasion aids, for if the Germans ever discovered that these packages were "loaded," they could stop Red Cross parcels from ever again entering a POW camp—packages whose foods and supplies were often the difference between life and death for POWs.

Winfrey borrowed once again from the practices of MI-9. By the Geneva Convention rules of war, POWs had the right to receive recreational devices approved by the holding power in parcels that would be carried postage-free by all nations. Reciprocity in this matter between the Allied and Axis powers was steadfastly maintained, as it meant that German POWs held in England,

Canada, and the United States would be accorded the same privileges. Britain's MI-9 had created fictitious humanitarian societies with such names as Lewis's Ltd., the British Local Ladies Comfort Society, the Order of St. John of Jerusalem, and the Lancashire Penny Fund, ostensibly Good Samaritan organizations through which they could, under the Geneva Convention, acceptably ship parcels to POW camps. England had thirty-six such agencies.

Winfrey found this guise equally suited for MIS-X objectives and chose the names the War Prisoner's Benefit Foundation and the Servicemen's Relief as America's benevolent pseudonyms. Because these organizations were wholly fictitious and would not, therefore, be soliciting contributions from the public, he was able to maintain complete control over their activities, since he would not have to register them with the state of Virginia or the IRS for permits and tax accountability.

Each of these "societies" would send three types of parcels: a "straight" food parcel, which would always be strictly humanitarian and contain no escape aids; a clothing parcel, which would be loaded with escape aids; and a recreational parcel, which would offer the greatest opportunity to transport escape aids, as they could be hidden within the papers and other materials of the game equipment.

Each society also had to appear absolutely legitimate. No one knew what checks the Gestapo would make when parcels entered Germany, and any oversights that might arouse suspicion could permanently shut down the operation. Each society's parcels, therefore, had to be composed of differently manufactured cardboard cartons, different labels, and different sealing tape, wrapping paper, and twine. Nothing could be used that might suggest the two groups were of the same origin. Even the glue on each society's labels was to be so distinct that under chemical analysis they would test differently. The

Germans had a reputation for painstaking vigilance, and Winfrey was determined to match them.

Regardless of how careful Winfrey was, the success of this critical facet of his operation would additionally depend on the cooperation of the U.S. Postal Service, for in order to maintain the appearance of legitimacy, the MIS-X societies would have to ship their parcels via the conventional postal service. Major General George Strong secured an appointment for Winfrey with the Postmaster General, James A. Farley, to discuss these special needs. Two concessions resulted from their meeting that had never before been granted to any organization by the postal service. First, all postmarks on MIS-X parcels would not be stamped by the usual and customary postal staff but would be personally affixed by either of only two senior supervisors. Second, all MIS-X mailbags would have a special tag in the routing clip indicating that only these two employees were authorized to handle and open MIS-X mail pouches.

It would be the job of these supervisors to place U.S. postmarks on the parcels they found in the specially marked bags and then feed the packages into the regular postal system. They would not know, however, the true origin or contents of the parcels—only that they bore the names of charitable societies that were presumably sending America's POWs goodwill materials.

And by March 1943, the materials were beginning to evolve. The nine craftsmen working in the shop had conquered the early problems with most of the wooden objects and were now turning out shaving brushes, shoe brushes, and Ping-Pong paddles that could be loaded and also pass Winfrey's critical examination. Paper products other than talcum powder containers were still proving difficult, however. The first batch of checkerboards appeared to be receptive to the heating treatment, but the second shipment failed to respond successfully. It was soon discovered that the two boards were from different manufacturers, and future purchases restricted to the one receptive brand resulted in checkerboards being added to the list of acceptable loading materials.

Satisfied that his technicians were progressing satisfactorily and that the shipments of parcels would be beginning in a matter of months, Winfrey decided that it was time to increase and expand the purchases that the three officers were making to accumulate stock for packages. Dried fruits, beans, canned milk, malt tablets, beef bouillon cubes, cocoa, salt, razors, razor blades, shaving soap, and canned sardines were now added to the list of supplies. In addition, Colonel Johnston, over his signature as a senior officer in the Military Intelligence Service's POW Branch, addressed a letter to the manufacturers of dried coffee, cube sugar, cigarettes, and soap. Stating that the War Department, in conjunction with the Ration Board, was granting a priority to two humanitarian societies—the Servicemen's Relief and the War Prisoner's Benefit Foundation—since their "good Christian" endeavors were directed toward U.S. POWs, he requested that these societies be permitted to purchase whatever goods they needed in whatever quantities they requested.

Arrangements were made with a Ben Franklin store in Baltimore to receive drop shipments in the names of the benefit societies, and the Ration Board, unwittingly cooperating because it believed in good faith that these societies were legitimate, waived the prescribed and ordinary requirement for ration stamps.

In addition to foods, materials would also soon be needed for the clothing parcels, so Colonel Russell Sweet, under the legitimate jurisdiction of his MIS-Y section of the POW Branch, submitted the first of several requisitions to the Quartermaster Corps for five hundred each of various-sized U.S. Army field jackets, olive drab shirts, trousers, shoes, socks, and wool gloves, as well as five hundred rubber heels for shoes, and sheets, blankets, and towels. His requisition stated that these materials were to be issued to the German POWs held at Fort Hunt and that the supplies would consequently be used, worn out, and eventually discarded. They were, in other words, to be considered expendable.

"Expendable" was the designation that Winfrey needed, for it would permit him to alter and load these articles and send them off to POWs without having to account for them to the Quartermaster Corps.

The requisition was approved without question, and the requested material arrived soon after from Fort Belvoir, located fifteen miles from Fort Hunt, and was received by the military police supply sergeant at the POW compound.

Around the same time came another arrival to 1142 who would finally complete Winfrey's technical staff. On April 20, 1943, Private First Class Maurice Hitchcock arrived eagerly at the railroad depot at Alexandria, Virginia. He had recently been a member of an infantry unit at Fort Devens, Massachusetts, where he had read a notice requesting experienced printers to volunteer for a special-duty assignment. Carrying sealed orders and given only a phone number—Temple 8141—by which to notify his new commanding officer of his arrival at the Alexandria depot, he was unaware of what specifically would be expected of him or where he would be stationed. Upon making his call, he was picked up by a staff car and delivered to 1142, where First Sergeant Alvin Yost assigned him to his quarters. He was then directed to report to Major Winfrey at the Warehouse.

As before, Winfrey lost little time on formalities. Briefing Hitchcock on MIS-X's mission and quickly introducing him to the other technicians, Winfrey marched Hitchcock to the far corner of the Warehouse where a new one-ton printing press had been assembled two weeks before. Wide-eyed, Hitchcock surveyed the room and saw a bank of shelves nearby holding several quart cans of multicolored inks, a makeup table containing three rows of trays holding type in German, French, and English, and a heavy-duty electric paper cutter flanked by steel bins filled with reams of assorted papers in a variety of sizes, colors, and thicknesses.

"Everything you need should be here," Winfrey said, looking at Hitchcock. "If it isn't, sing out. Now, can you work here?"

"Yes, sir!" Hitchcock exclaimed, his face ablaze with delight. "It's a printer's dream. Hell, I could even counterfeit money here if you wanted me to!"

With a twinkle in his eye, Winfrey responded, "In time, my boy, in time."[1] Then he left the man to acquaint himself with his new work area.

The technical and correspondence sections were now fully staffed, and as if on cue, MIS-X received its first letter, or "signal," from a U.S. POW. It had first arrived at MI-9, London, and was forwarded to the Pentagon communications center via a coded telex, whereupon Colonel Jones immediately sent it to 1142 by courier. Master Sergeant Silvio A. Bedini, chief cryptoanalyst in the Creamery, was given the letter, decoded it, and excitedly relayed its contents to Winfrey: "Lieut. Col. Albert P. Clark SAO [Senior American Officer] with 87 officers PD [period] Send instructions PD."

Winfrey anxiously checked the POW list supplied to the Prisoner of War Branch by the International Red Cross in Geneva and discovered that a Lieutenant Colonel Albert P. Clark, Jr., had been a fighter pilot with the Thirty-first Fighter Group and had been the second U.S. airman to be downed in the war, shot down on July 26, 1942, while participating in a fighter sweep over the Abbeville Airfield in France with the Royal Canadian Air Force.[2] The records showed that he was currently being held captive with approximately 12,000 English airmen in the North Compound of Stalag Luft III in Sagan, Germany (now part of Poland), where the British escape and evasion committee inside the camp had advised MI-9 of Clark's arrival. Under instructions from Brigadier Crockatt, Clark had been taught British code 3.

Because Clark had been trained in the letter code by the British and did not have a preexisting contact in the United States, his signal was received by MI-9, who, after forwarding it to Jones, wrote an acknowledgment to Clark: "Air Force doing great work PD Instructions will follow PD."[3]

Communication had finally been made with an American POW, and the need for MIS-X to be up and running was now growing imperative.

In a matter of weeks it would become urgent.

5

———✗———✗———

WE DELIVER

IN EARLY MAY 1943, one of the twenty-four women sorting mail at the New York censor's office stopped suddenly when she spied a return address of POW Camp 64, Schubin, Poland. Working under Colonel Fred W. Siegel, chief U.S. military censor, it was her job to examine incoming mail and pull all letters and packages with a return address of a POW camp in Europe. She was to put these items in an overhead routing box, which a messenger emptied every hour. She knew the letters were important but did not know why. This being her first "find," she became excited. Jumping up from her desk, she raced across the hall to Colonel Siegel's office. "I found one," she cried out, brushing past the colonel's secretary and handing him the letter.

"Indeed you have, young lady. Thank you, and keep a sharp eye out for the next one," Siegel told her.

She heard a tone of dismissal in his voice and was slightly miffed at the apparent minimizing of her discovery.

As she left the office, however, Siegel pushed a desk button that summoned his assistant, Captain Paul Yarck, from the adjoining office. "Paul," he said as the captain entered, "we have two this morning for 1142. I'm going to call Captain Churchill. I know he will be happy to know they've started coming through. Get these letters into a security envelope and on the afternoon courier plane to Washington."

Alerted that two letters were en route, chief briefer Creighton Churchill advised Winfrey and then dispatched an officer to meet the courier plane at Bolling Field Air Force Base, five miles south of Washington on the Maryland side of the Potomac River. Thirty minutes after the letters arrived at 1142, Bedini deciphered the first message: "Moving soon PD Need maps compass and money PD."[1] It was signed "Hobo," and the return address was Oflag 64, a ground-force officers' camp in Schubin, Poland.

Winfrey was ecstatic: "Hobo" was a code name that MIS-X had assigned to a code user. This message, therefore, was the first evidence that the efforts of his briefers in training airmen to be active POWs were paying off.

After 1800 hours, Bedini completed decoding the second message, but its contents puzzled him. Message in hand, he left the Creamery and crossed over to the Warehouse just as Winfrey was about to leave. Winfrey read it aloud: "Give this message to address below PD Send part diagram 220 direct and alternating PD John C. Bowman 2900 Nichols Street San Diego, Calif PD Signed: Boxer."[2]

As with previous messages, this one had been written in British code 3, which the sender no doubt had been taught by a British CU. A check revealed the writer to be Lieutenant Horace Dale Bowman of the Thirty-third Bomb Group. Before any attempt was made to contact John Bowman in San Diego, a security check would have to be done.

The next morning, Winfrey briefed Colonel Johnston on the two signals and requested that he make contact with J. Edgar Hoover of the FBI for assistance in a background check on John Bowman.

While he was waiting for the check to come through, Winfrey turned his attention to the first message. A study of the Red Cross list of POWs revealed the sender to be Lieutenant Keith Wilson, a U.S. pilot in the Fifteenth Air Force, operating out of North Africa. Apparently, from his message, the prisoners were going to be moved from Oflag 64 to another camp, and they wanted to attempt an escape before or during the movement. Winfrey had planned to ship his first humanitarian parcels near the first of June in order to accustom the German censors to seeing the labels of the fictitious American societies. After a few hundred had been spread through various camps, he would then start enclosing some escape materials in the packages. But this coded letter from Wilson clearly required immediate action, and Winfrey would have to abandon both his schedule and his precautions. Following a discussion with Johnston at the Pentagon, who confirmed Winfrey's concern, Winfrey decided to act on the messages at once.

Summoning his three officers and ten technicians to a meeting in the Warehouse, Winfrey reviewed the two signals. Next to him, on his desk, was a plaque that Sergeant Harris had made for him a month before that read "UNCLE SAM'S GENERAL MERC—WE DELIVER." Completing the briefing of his crew, Winfrey pointed to the plaque and said, "We are opening the store thirty days early."

Excited and anxious, the crew set about unpacking cardboard parcel cartons and checking labels, sealing tape, twine, and wrapping paper to ensure that none of the shipping materials overlapped between the two humanitarian societies. Because POWs were surviving on subsistence diets and because rations could be used to bribe the German guards, Winfrey decided that a food parcel from the Servicemen's Relief would be the first type of package sent out by MIS-X and that a total of twenty parcels would be in the first shipment. When all the parcels were assembled and checked, Winfrey once more reviewed the contents from his list, which had been compiled to ensure compliance with the Geneva Convention's requirement that humanitarian packages not weigh more than eleven pounds. Satisfied that all was in order, Winfrey called out each item and Corporal Carl Peterson, in charge of Warehouse shipping and receiving, laid them out on the long shipping counter:

1 carton of cigarettes
3 boxes of safety matches
1 1-pound box of cubed sugar
1 1-pound can of cocoa
4 4-ounce cans of condensed milk
1 12-ounce box of oatmeal
1 pound of rice
1 8-ounce pack of dried apples, of apricots, and
    of prunes
2 4-ounce cans of corned beef
2 4-ounce jars of instant coffee
2 packages of chewing gum
1 shaving razor
2 packages of razor blades
1 shaving brush
1 bar of shaving soap

Peterson carefully filled each parcel as Winfrey read off the list, pushing each completed package down the counter, until they came to the nineteenth one. This was the one that Winfrey had designated would be "loaded" and sent to Lieutenant Keith Wilson. Here, instead of the straight shaving brush, a special one was brought out from the shop area. The handle end had been cut off with a gigili saw, the handle hollowed with a router, and five tissue maps were placed in the bottom of the handle with five small compasses resting on top of them. Ten Reichmark bills were then placed along the sides of the handle and folded so as to press against the compasses to keep them from rattling. The handle was then glued back together, sanded, and varnished until any signs of tampering were removed.

The twentieth package was left open, as it was to be sent to Lieutenant Bowman upon approval from the FBI and identification of the requested item from his brother.

The next morning, Colonel Johnston phoned 1142 and advised Winfrey that the FBI had reported that Horace Dale Bowman's brother, John Bowman, was an engineer in the aircraft industry and held a sensitive position that had previously been checked by the bureau. He was considered a good risk and a good worker. Johnston then advised Winfrey that he was ordering Captain John Starr to board a plane for the West Coast. Dressed in civilian clothes and posing as a representative from some publicly known humanitarian society, Starr was to make contact with John Bowman and obtain from him part 220, whatever that was. Starr was to advise Bowman only that his brother had requested the part, that Starr would see to it that it was passed on to his brother, and that absolute secrecy was essential. John Bowman would not know specifically how the part would be delivered nor how Starr had received the request.[3]

Starr arrived in San Diego and located Bowman, who readily identified part 220 as a diagram for a radio transmitter that he and his younger brother had been building before the war. They were, it turned out, amateur radio buffs.

The diagram was carefully inserted in a shoe brush, the shaving brush and shaving soap were removed from the parcel and the shoe brush and a can of polish were enclosed instead.[4] Then Winfrey directed Starr to prepare and send a coded letter to "Hobo" and "Boxer" at Oflag 64, advising them that their parcels were en route and that the latter should "break wooden objects." With that, labels were attached to the twenty parcels—eighteen names picked at random from a Red Cross list of POWs at Oflag 64, and the last two addressed to Lieutenant Keith Wilson and Lieutenant Horace Dale Bowman.

Peterson then took the tray of censor's stamps from the Warehouse's office safe and stamped each parcel half on the label and half on the wrapper. The circular stamps carried the words "U.S. Censor" and had the censor's number. To avoid suspicion, the stamps were not numbered consecutively but ranged from 1364 to 12140. The parcels were then stuffed into five regular U.S. mail sacks, and these were then secured with the coded red routing tags identifying them as special parcels to be handled solely by the preapproved inspectors at the Baltimore post office. The mailbags were then taken from 1142 by an MIS-X officer wearing civilian clothes and driving a nonmilitary automobile.

The first straight and loaded parcels had now been sent, and the crew could do nothing more but cross their fingers and hope.

But the die was cast and the pattern set. There would hereafter be no rest. Winfrey was determined to start shipping regularly.

6

—✗———✗—

CODE LETTER FROM POLAND

WHEN THE TWENTY PARCELS left 1142 for Oflag 64,
they followed a course that most subsequent mailings
would follow.

Virtually all mail leaving America for U.S. POWs in
Germany went first to the neutral countries of
Switzerland, Sweden, or Portugal, where it was sorted
out in a warehouse and readied for rail connection to
Germany. The Germans then sent boxcars to the bor-
ders, which were loaded in a manner that would make
delivery expedient and efficient to the camps throughout
Germany.

Upon their arrival at the camps, the parcels would
have to pass the German censors. Once inside the
camps, any contraband received would have to be hidden from German barracks inspections as well as the
general awareness of the POWs.

To accomplish this and oversee the daily operation of
the camp, the senior ranking POW in an officers' camp,
regardless of his nationality, automatically assumed responsibility for camp routine and, as camp commanding

officer (CO), reported directly to the German commandant of the compound. (In enlisted men's camps, the
leader was elected by the POWs and was given the title
Man of Confidence, or MOC.)

At the time the twenty parcels were making their way
to Oflag 64, the CO of the camp was James D. Alger, a
thirty-three-year-old lieutenant colonel who had been in
the army for ten years and had been captured in North
Africa on February 15, 1943, at Sidi-bou-Zid. A member
of the First Armored Regiment, First Armored Division,
Alger had been briefed in escape and evasion by MIS-
X.[1] His responsibility now was to put that knowledge to
use effectively for the protection and betterment of the
three hundred American officers presently under his
command as POWs at Oflag 64.

To assist him in his administration of the camp, Alger
followed the practice of establishing a military organization within barbed-wire confines and appointed other
POWs to the few staff positions necessary for handling
the duties of his small camp. These staff positions included an adjutant, and mess, laundry, and parcels
(mail) officers.

The adjutant served as an administrative assistant to
the CO. He maintained a list of all personnel in the
camp and all personnel in the hospital; he was responsible for making sure that the camp history was recorded
in a log and was the liaison between the commanding
officer and the POWs.

The mess officer made sure that everyone equally
shared all food arriving in the camp from any source—
German, American, Red Cross, and others. As food was
prepared by the POWs themselves, the mess officer also
was in charge of ensuring that the Germans provided sufficient eating utensils and cooking equipment and cooking fuel for the camp.

The laundry officer arranged for the camp laundry to
be handled by the wives of some of the German guards,

who were delighted to obtain the extra income, and collected money from the POWs to pay for this service.

The parcels officer was always on hand when mail was received in the camp *Vorlager* (receiving area) to ensure that the Germans did not pilfer any POW supplies during mail censoring.

In addition to these routine camp positions, and in keeping with the directive that a POW was to harass, confuse, and disrupt his captors' daily routine and "make every effort to regain [his] freedom and rejoin [his] command," Alger appointed an officer to oversee the functions of the camp's covert escape and evasion committee.

To head the E&E committee, Alger selected Lieutenant Colonel John H. Van Vliet, a West Point graduate who had been captured in North Africa two days after Alger while serving with the 168th Infantry, Thirty-fourth Division. Thirty years old, Van Vliet had already had eight years of active duty and had also been briefed by MIS-X. As head of the camp escape committee, he would hereafter be known only as "Big X."[2] His true identity would be shielded from most of the camp personnel, and his actual activities would not even be known to Alger, so that the CO could face the German commandant with a clear conscience during times of German suspicion.

The "Big X" had to be a strong leader, capable of masterminding deception with flawless control. To assist in organizing camp resistance through escape efforts, he selected a staff to head up the various facets of the escape organization:

Security	Finances
Codes	Nuisances
Maps	Tunnels
Forgery	News
Gadgets	Tailoring
Intelligence	Parcels

Each of these special branches of the escape committee was carefully compartmentalized, with separate lines of communication directly to "Big X." Thus, the men who operated the radio or received the code messages did not know who was working in the factories, who was tunneling, who was taking part in gathering intelligence, and so on. To oversee the successful coordination of these subcommittees and ensure their secrecy, the chairman of the escape and evasion committee appointed an executive officer to head the security branch of his staff.

To provide protection for his covert activities, Van Vliet would need a security officer, who would be known as "Big S." He was responsible for obtaining detailed information regarding the comings and goings of the German camp personnel—who came into the camp, who left it, at what time, by what schedules—and though he had, of necessity, general knowledge of what escape activities were in progress, even he would not necessarily know specifics. Security was never taken for granted. To fill the position, he chose Lieutenant Colonel John K. Waters, a West Point graduate who was also Lieutenant General George S. Patton's son-in-law and had been captured on February 14, 1943, while a member of the First Armored Regiment, First Armored Division. As "Big S," Waters would be in charge of all camp security and provide cover for camp escape activities.[3]

It was a general security principle to concentrate a particular type of escape activity in a given barracks or cluster of barracks—called a "block"—to reduce physical traffic and prevent the Germans from noting patterns of movement or conspicuous concentrations of POWs. Each of these blocks also had its own security officer, and the "Big S" was responsible for informing that officer as to when escape work was to start in his block and when it was to stop.

The POWs in charge of maps and of forgery respectively kept an update on regional maps to be used by escapers and oversaw the preparation of all forged documents necessary for an escapee's transition through the German countryside and checkpoints. The gadgets unit built compasses and other escape devices on-site; the intelligence crew was responsible for obtaining information of military importance from the German guards and maintenance crew. Finances kept, hid, and dispensed all Reichmarks that were sent to the camp from MIS-X; the nuisances group created distractions during escapes, tunnel digging, or other escape-related activities, and the tunnels unit dug the tunnels. Tailoring created the clothing needed by escapees when they entered the "outside" world; the news crew relayed news of the war as monitored from BBC broadcasts; and the parcels group received and ensured the safe delivery of the packages that arrived on the trains from neutral countries.

Of all camp covert activities, radio operation was veiled in the most complete secrecy. The entire operation was conducted in one room in a barracks, and all appropriate personnel lived in that one room—technicians, shorthand men, and the man who hid the radio. While only one person could operate the radio at a time, each member of the radio staff was responsible for standing lookout whenever the radio was in use. One person stood at the window of the room, one stood at the door, and one stood at each of the two entries to the barracks, watching the "stooges" outside for any indication of approaching German guards. Even fellow POWs were never to know who worked the radio or where it was.

News of the war could understandably be an invaluable morale booster to POWs. Knowledge of German forces repelled, cities overrun, or forthcoming Allied invasion plans could elevate a POW's spirit, which might otherwise be broken through the trauma of capture and fear of the unknown. News coming into the camp

stances, alerted him to keep an eye out for the two packages addressed to Wilson and Bowman and advise Van Vliet immediately through messenger of their arrival at the camp.

In the last week of June 1943, the loaded parcels arrived at Oflag 64, and Dicks and his three assistants—Lieutenant Amon Carter, Lieutenant Royal Lee, and Lieutenant Harry T. Schultz—were on hand at the *Vorlager,* where they had been anxiously on the lookout for several weeks. These parcels stood out from the ordinary mail as they were different in size and packaging—the Red Cross parcels, for example, were wooden and strapped with metal bindings and MIS-X's Servicemen's Relief parcels were made of cardboard, wrapped in brown paper, and secured with hemp twine.

Dicks was not permitted to handle the packages at this point but could only monitor the way they were handled and protect them against theft. The German guards took up the parcels and placed them five at a time on a table for review by the censor. The metal bindings of the Red Cross parcels were removed and kept, as these could be used by the POWs to make saws or other escape materials. Each package was then inspected by the censor for evidence of contraband. Dicks, not aware of what was hidden inside the parcels or what items contained the hidden materials, watched nervously as the tin of shoe polish and bar of shaving soap in the Servicemen's Relief parcels were opened and poked randomly with a needle in search of concealed items. As the American E&E efforts were still in their infancy, however, the Germans had no reason to suspect foul play in the humanitarian packages arriving into the camp, and the censor quickly passed Bowman and Wilson's parcels with little more than this routine and uneventful inspection. The hollowed-out and loaded shaving brush and shoe brush were never suspected.

Alger, Van Vliet, Waters, Wilson, and Bowman were

all waiting in Bowman's quarters when Dicks arrived with the two packages addressed to Wilson and Bowman. Waters had posted security sentinels—stooges, as they were called—to watch for any unauthorized personnel (German and POW), and the packages were then opened and the contents strewn on one of the double bunks. None of the officers had ever received loaded articles, and they were all initially confused as foodstuffs rolled out along with a perfectly normal-looking shoe brush and shaving brush. The coded messages they had received had said to "break all wooden objects,"[4] but nothing looked as if it had been tampered with or was in any but manufacturer's condition.

Fighting back disappointment, they picked up the two brushes and decided to follow their instructions anyway. Breaking open the shaving brush, they were astonished as five small compasses and a wad of German Reichmarks fell out. For a moment they remained quiet, overwhelmed by what had been accomplished. Finally, Waters looked at everyone and said, "Manna from heaven."

Several months later, Bowman, having since obtained the parts to build the radio from the diagram he had received in the loaded shoe brush, wrote once again to his brother in San Diego, advising him in a noncoded but carefully written letter that the radio they had worked on together during their ham radio days was now in service.

And MIS-X, "Uncle Sam's Mercantile," had successfully delivered its first shipment to assist U.S. POWs—unbeknownst to virtually everyone except the handful of men working in a remote corner of 1142 in Alexandria, Virginia.

7

×————×

INSIDE
STALAG LUFT III

IN MAY 1943 the Creamery received a series of letter codes that were identified as having been sent from Stalag Luft III in Sagan, Germany, that were passed immediately to Winfrey because of their obvious urgency.[1]

Located about eighty miles southeast of Berlin, Stalag Luft III was an air officers' camp established by German Field Marshal Hermann Göring, who had been a German air ace in World War I. A firm believer in the superiority and chivalry of the air force, Göring convinced Hitler that a special camaraderie existed between airmen and that the Luftwaffe (German air force) should guard all Allied air POWs, while the Wehrmacht (German infantry) could guard the ground-force POWs. Separate camps were therefore to be created to accommodate this plan of segregating air force personnel from ground forces.

Shortly after its completion in March 1942, Americans began arriving in Stalag Luft III and were assigned to the East Compound, where two thousand British POWs were already quartered. The senior British officer, Group Captain Martin Massey, welcomed the entering

U.S. POWs as they arrived, and as it would still be some time before the Americans received Red Cross parcels, he ordered that the English fliers share their rations with the U.S. POWs to prevent starvation, which would have resulted from attempting to survive on the German rations provided.

As the air war over Europe intensified, so did the flow of British and American POW airmen into Stalag Luft III. The Germans had vastly underestimated the number of prisoners that would be taken, and they soon realized that additional compounds would have to be added to the camp. In January 1943, therefore, they began construction of what would come to be known as North Compound, which was to be located north of East Compound and designed to hold twenty-five hundred prisoners.

In April 1943 North Compound was completed, and the British and American POWs held in East Compound were moved in. The vacated East Compound was then filled with British airmen being transferred to Stalag Luft III from ground-force camps (Oflagen) throughout Germany, in compliance with Göring's orders.

Once they were moved into North Compound, the British and U.S. POWs resumed their escape activities, and the U.S. POWs began sending the coded messages that Winfrey now held in his hands.

One of the coded messages read: "Fort emerg forward hatch not working right PD Many can't get out PD."[2] "Fort" referred to the B-17 Flying Fortress, and the signal was advising that the forward hatch of the plane was jamming, preventing the crew from evacuating in emergencies. Upon receiving the code, Winfrey forwarded the message to Major General George Strong, who telephoned the air force headquarters at Wright-Patterson Field, in Dayton, Ohio. Twenty-four hours after it received the information, air force intelligence had notified every wing of the army/air force to correct the equipment malfunction.

Another code read: "Tell fellows avoid *Tours* PD Chances poor inside Germany PD."[3] Its intent was to alert escapees and evaders to avoid passing through the city of Tours, France, as it had highly policed control checkpoints.

Two other messages advised that a "bogus Red Cross" official was being used by the Germans to extract information from unsuspecting POWs and that prisoners interrogated at various Dulagen were giving the Germans too much information as a result of the Germans subjecting them to solitary confinement.

These were important signals for MIS-X, as they indicated that the letter code system could be used successfully to convey critical intelligence information.

One of the signals Winfrey received in the cluster of letter codes, however, was directly pertinent to his MIS-X activities, as it was a request for supplies: "Send food coupons, money, border maps PD "Gen" on help PD M D G PD."[4] As "Gen" was British for "information," Winfrey knew that, in addition to aids, this message was a request for any information on escape routes, control points, and other relevant material. As one of the other messages in this series indicated that the initial *G* at the end of the code stood for Goodrich, Winfrey could identify the sender as Colonel Charles "Rojo" Goodrich, an airman who, upon his arrival in the camp, had succeeded Lieutenant Colonel Albert Clark as the senior American officer (SAO).

Winfrey viewed Goodrich's message as good news. A request for aids that he recognized as essential for moving an escapee through a police state such as Germany, it confirmed that the camps were getting organized and becoming escape-minded.

Carrying Goodrich's signal in hand, Winfrey ran from

his small office to the shop area to check on its progress. After reviewing the escape gadgets on hand with Warehouse foreman Peterson, Winfrey next made his way to the far corner to inspect the counterfeit documents coming off Hitchcock's press. Confirming that the materials looked authentic, Winfrey hurried back to his office and, before even reaching the door, called out to Corporal Paul Huss, his clerk typist, "Let's get up fifty parcels with ten to be loaded. They go to Colonel Goodrich at North Compound at Stalag Luft III. Check with Sergeant Bedini for names at random on the straight parcels, and let's use the War Prisoner's Benefit Foundation this time. Also, ask Captain Churchill to send off a letter to Goodrich alerting him as to the ten names on the hot parcels."

The Warehouse now became a beehive of activity, as this was to be the largest MIS-X shipment to date. There would be thirty straight food parcels and ten straight game parcels; the remaining ten game parcels would be loaded with escape aids.

The shipping cartons were prepared by Hitchcock and Peterson, who then began the painstaking process of laying out the various materials for the forty straight parcels. Every precaution had to be taken to ensure that the straight items for the War Prisoner's Benefit Foundation were not inadvertently mixed with those that would be used for the Servicemen's Relief group. Then the packages were to be filled, checked, wrapped, tied, addressed, and set aside before the loaded packages would be begun.

As Winfrey stood by with his clipboard, the loaded parcels were prepared. Each loaded item had an adhesive label on it with a number that identified the contraband it contained. As each item was placed in a parcel, the adhesive label was removed, and as either Peterson or Hitchcock called the number out, Winfrey would note it on his clipboard opposite the receiving

POW's name and camp address so that he would always know who received what and where it went.

The escape aids that were to be sent in this shipment would include a crystal radio set concealed in a cribbage board; twenty half-inch compasses wrapped in cotton inside twenty individual chess pieces; and ten counterfeit German work permits (the names and dates of which were left blank), travel permits, and five hundred legitimate Reichmarks (in ten-Mark denominations) hidden in the chessboard itself. In addition, four checkerboards carried ten sets of ration coupons each—to be used in cafés—and five pairs of Ping-Pong paddles carried an assortment of tissue paper maps of the area around Sagan and the German-Swiss border.

It took most of the day to ready this large shipment for delivery to Stalag Luft III. When Winfrey was satisfied that everything was acceptable, each parcel was stamped with a censor's stamp, and a postal cancellation mark was placed on each, indicating Baltimore, Maryland, as the point of origin. The parcels were then bagged five to a mail sack, the special routing tag was attached to each bag, and an MIS-X officer, dressed in mufti, took the parcels to the Baltimore Post office in his own private vehicle, where they would enter the conventional postal system. The officer would be allowed extra gasoline ration stamps and be paid a mileage rate for the hundred-mile round trip.

Lieutenant Colonel Leslie Winterbottom, the British adviser still on hand at the Creamery, working on developing American codes with Sergeant Bedini, stood in the Warehouse talking to Winfrey as the last parcel was bagged and locked. "It looks good, Bob. Very good, indeed. Your men have done their work well, and mark my words—these parcels will sail through German censorship as easily as lying in the arms of Morpheus."

But Winfrey's mind was following a different course. MIS-X's mission was to supply escape devices to American POWs. As a conscientious, professional engineer, his concern was the possibility of an unforeseen oversight occurring somewhere in his preparations. If the curiosity of a German censor were aroused, the entire operation would be blown—and while the consequences of losing aid shipments to U.S. POWs would be tragic, imperiling Britain's MI-9 activities because of an American foul-up would be inexcusable.

"I hope you're right, Leslie," Winfrey said, "for the sake of us all." Then, with a quiet sigh, he resigned himself to the fact that all that could be done had been done.

Winfrey and Winterbottom then turned from the Warehouse and walked back to the front office, arriving just as Sergeant Bedini was knocking on the door with an uncoded postcard that had just come from the Pentagon.

"I've got a cutie," Bedini exclaimed, handing the signal to Winfrey, who scanned the message, grinned, and then read it out loud to Winterbottom:

Mr. F. B. Eyers
6 Pennsylvania St.
Washington, D.C.

Dear Uncle Fred,
I just wanted to tell you I am OK. We were shot down over France, and I am a POW at Stalag 17-B at Krems, Austria. Please tell my Uncle Sam.

S/Sgt. Edward T. Cross
Stalag 17-B

Bedini explained that the card had been originally delivered to the main office of the Federal Bureau of Investigation, where they had correctly identified the sender's intent and forwarded it to the POW Branch at the Pentagon. Winfrey was understandably impressed with the writer's ingenuity, and shortly after receiving the card, he suggested to Captain Creighton Churchill, the chief briefer, that a coded message be sent to Stalag 17-B recommending that Cross be made a CU.

Winfrey realized that a similar display of ingenuity would be required of the POWs at Stalag Luft III. The coded letters to Goodrich, notifying him that the parcels were on their way, had been sent by air mail and would arrive in Stalag Luft III within three weeks—but the packages would take five to six weeks, traveling by convoy across the Atlantic Ocean.

The standard Red Cross food parcel was similar to
the "loaded" food parcels sent by MIS-X. *(American
Red Cross)*

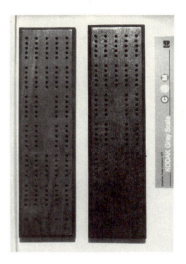

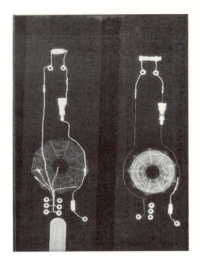

Two ⅝-inch-thick cribbage boards "loaded" by MIS-X. *(Silvio A. Bedini)*

X ray of cribbage boards reveals radios sent to POWs by MIS-X. *(Silvio A. Bedini)*

Game board used as carrier for escape aids. Wooden sides were hollowed to hide maps and money. *(Author's collection)*

Chessboard top was steamed off, and a cavity was created in the layered paper to carry money, maps, and forged documents. *(Silvio A. Bedini)*

8

---×------×---

ESCAPE AND EVADE

ABOUT 10:00 A.M. ON a warm mid-August morning, Captain Creighton Churchill, chief briefer at the Creamery, hurried over to Winfrey's office. "Robbie," Churchill exclaimed upon seeing him, "they made it! And we get a bonus." He then handed Winfrey a signal that had arrived at 1142 that morning: "Ten hot parcels received PD Repats Glass and Herrington have details PD." The message, signed by Colonel Goodrich, established that the parcels MIS-X had recently sent had indeed arrived at Stalag Luft III. But even more significant was the second part of the message, which revealed that the POWs were now using repatriates as a means of communication. Severely wounded fighting men whom the Germans submitted to an international medical board would be sent home, or repatriated, if three of the four examining physicians concurred that the POW was beyond useful military service. Glass and Herrington would be the first American repatriates, and Goodrich's signal indicated that they were "hot."

"This is great," Winfrey said excitedly. "Holt will grab them for us and milk them dry."

Lieutenant Colonel W. Stull Holt was well known to Winfrey, as they had met one another in England while serving on Major General Carl Spaatz's staff. A World War I pilot in the U.S. Army Air Corps, Holt was teaching history at Johns Hopkins University when World War II broke out, and he volunteered to serve in the war effort. Appointed to Spaatz's staff, Holt was subsequently detached to serve as liaison between Spaatz and MI-9. His orders from Spaatz read as follows:

> To study and perfect the escape and evasion techniques into a program to be used by the American briefers as they indoctrinated U.S. Army air and ground force troops prior to combat; the proper employment of this indoctrination; how to behave if captured; what to say during interrogation; how to escape from a POW camp; and the selection of certain individuals in combat units who would be taught a secret letter code to be employed if captured by the enemy. . . . Finally, you will identify the names and if possible, addresses of all civilians on the continent who aided and abetted Allied escapers and evaders and to what extent aid was extended.[1]

Holt reported directly to Spaatz only, during the entire war, but would convey his findings to both MI-9 and MIS-X.

From the moment he took on his assignment, Holt worked around the clock, personally reviewing and initialing every escape and evasion report coming out of the European theater and reporting his findings to Spaatz. He studied the reports to learn what circumstances had assisted or hampered escape and evasion efforts, as well as any inconsistencies, details, or seemingly insignificant events that would shed more light on Axis activities. Where information in a report raised a question in his mind or where it seemed particularly pertinent, Holt would arrange to meet the POW and interview the escaper or evader personally for clarification.

As tireless and conscientious as Winfrey, Holt had a disposition that made him an ideal liaison between British formality and Yankee aggressiveness. He was quickly accepted by the British, and set up his office at MI-9's operational site, Camp 20, a few miles outside of London.

In mid-September Holt, having seen the paperwork on Glass and Herrington and recognized their importance as the first American repatriates, sent the following cable to Colonel Catesby ap Jones at the Pentagon: "Glass and Herrington to be met upon arrival and escorted to my office for de-briefing. Their details follow."

Ten days later, Holt's multipaged interrogation report arrived at 1142 via air courier. Winfrey read it excitedly, as it was the first report his office had received containing firsthand information regarding treatment of U.S. POWs in a German POW camp:

> 1st Lt. Albert W. Glass, bombadier, shot down over North Sea and 1st Lt. Glen M. Herrington, navigator, shot down over Saint-Nazaire, France. Both received serious wounds and were treated by German doctors. Both were sent to Stalag Luft III to recuperate in camp hosp. Both are physically beyond military service due to the disabling wounds.
>
> Upon passing the combined medical board, there was a three-week wait for the transfer to begin. Col. Goodrich had them come to his room in the barracks where he and Lt. Col. Albert P. Clark had them memorize details which were to be repeated only to an MIS-X officer.
>
> There are about 2,500 officers at Stalag Luft III, of which 152 are American. Morale is high,

discipline is good, escape activities are extensive, and leadership is aggressive.

British Group Captain Massey is the Senior Allied Officer serving as Camp Commander. The Germans, believing that the prisoners' own Allied officers can better control the POWs, recognize the senior officer, and permit him to appoint his own personal staff to assist in the daily routine.[2]

The most invaluable information that Holt obtained from Glass and Herrington was the actual description of a POW camp escape committee, in which the Americans and British were working cooperatively. As Holt related:

Both Glass and Herrington were surprised to learn from Goodrich and Clark the extent of the Escape Committee.

Group Captain Massey appointed Squadron Leader Roger Bushell as Chairman of the "X" Committee [the conventional term for the escape committee], and he is the authority for all covert functions within the camp. He is known as "Big X." He, too, has men to assist him in these operations. The first is security who is called "Big S." The Americans have integrated with the British and Bushell has selected Lt. Col. Albert P. Clark to be the "Big S" in charge of all camp security.

The British have a radio and listen to the BBC news each night. This is taken down in shorthand by a former court reporter who reads the news to the men in each barracks.

There are departments called "factories" where members of the Committee make compasses, reproduce maps; tailors alter and dye uniforms to resemble civilian clothes. Men with the artistic touch forge ID cards, travel permits, and work passes.

The nuisance group creates diversions on cue, such as sham fights, to distract the guards' attention during times of crises. There are tunnelers and three long tunnels known as Tom, Dick, & Harry are being dug for a mass escape.

Col. Goodrich said there were two CUs in the camp beside himself, but they are known only to himself, "Big X," and "Big S." Messages are being received in the letter codes with no apparent suspicion by the Germans. Col. McNichols is the Chief Parcel Officer and so far sees no suspicion on the part of the German censors who are always sergeants. The ten special parcels were received without absconding them.

Col. Goodrich says escapists can get out fairly easy but the problem is staying out. Germany is a police state where all civilians are required to carry ID and have papers to move about, from town to town, to go to work, and ration coupons at cafés. Controls are set up at all rail stations, on moving trains, and at all roads of consequence.

What are most needed are civilian clothes with European cut. Money should be in 1, 2, 5, and 10 Mark notes. Printed passes, travel permits, ID card papers (leave all names and dates blank). Wiring diagram and radio parts. Solder, small tools, electric wire, writing ink, rubber heels, patterns for men's suits, candles, hair clippers, files, hacksaws, razors, and blades and maps.

Many escapes have taken place but most are returned to the camp within a day or two. The main obstacle is the Hitler Youth, teen-age boys who swarm the woods and roads in the hundreds when an escape alarm is sounded. When one spots a suspicious person, he blows a whistle and droves of boys surround an escaper in minutes. They are all armed with heavy walking sticks and use them as clubs.[3]

Glass and Herrington then closed their report to Holt by reciting the names of POWs who had been in other camps prior to arriving at Stalag Luft III.

Winfrey set the report down and breathed easily for the first time since the MIS-X shipments had begun. The parcels were getting through, the Germans were not suspicious, and the secret letter codes were working. MIS-X was on track.

Holt, meanwhile, had by now amassed considerable information on escape and evasion methods through his interviews with British evaders from Dunkirk and the trickle of escapers that had come from POW camps. Knowing that his research would be invaluable to Winfrey and Crockatt in training their briefers, Holt wrote out his findings, containing recommended policies and actual escape and evasion anecdotes, and sent memos to MI-9 and MIS-X for their use. These reports had arrived in Winfrey's office about the same time as the report on Glass and Herrington, and Winfrey turned to Holt's recommendations now:

1. Do not carry personal papers on your person. The address on letters from home carry your military unit and address.
2. If captured, give only your name, rank, and serial number as prescribed by the Geneva Convention. Beware of enemy personnel impersonating Red Cross officials who tell you that you will not be declared a POW until you complete a form which asks for your military unit, address, name of CO, and members of your crew.

3. Evade if possible before capture. Escape is most likely to be easiest if done early.
4. Stay off well-traveled roads to avoid transit control points.
5. Seek out farmers in remote areas for food and civilian clothes. *Memorize* their names. *Do not* write them to be carried on your person.
6. Make every effort to keep yourself clean and neat to avoid suspicion and attracting attention.
7. Discreet inquiries may be made at cafés and coffee houses.
8. BE AN ESCAPER—NOT AN EVADER
   A recent American evader who had been successful in making his way south, through Germany, after being shot down, crossed the frontier into Switzerland. He told Swiss officials he was an evader instead of saying he had escaped from German hands. He was interned for the duration. (Under the Geneva Convention, an escaper could be returned to his homeland.)
9. LOOK BEFORE YOU LEAP
   An evader was crossing a bridge at dusk and did not notice the sentries on the far side until he was almost across, and it was too late to turn back. He walked up to the sentry and appeared to search for his papers, feigning surprise when he did not find them. He then turned to walk back. The sentry let him go on. But it was obviously dangerous to take such a chance.
10. CROSSING THE PYRENEES
    Several escapers, in late spring, suffered severely from frostbite. In one instance, a toe was amputated. In another, frostbite was so

severe the man would never walk correctly again. Airmen were apt to wear what they preferred, but low oxford shoes and cotton socks were to be avoided when flying missions.

11. USING HIS HEAD

One successful escaper showed good judgment in getting through a RR station control by watching for his chance and walking through the baggage room with a group of French workmen. He had no identity papers or travel permit.

12. Another offered his seat in a railway carriage to a German officer who was standing. The officer gratefully accepted and later, when the control guard came through and asked for the evader's papers, the officer waved him on. The evader had no papers.

13. ONE O'CLOCK

"Just as the train was coming in, a guard challenged me for my papers. When it seemed I would miss the train, I pointed out to him that his fly was open. While he was busy buttoning up, I jumped on the moving train." (One o'Clock, American—Star of India, British)

14. DISGUISE

An escaper traveling on a train found a Fascist cap in the carriage and hung it up behind him. The other passengers accepted him as Italian, as did the control officer.

15. BE INVENTIVE

Another escaper on a train in Toulouse states, "When the control officer came through the carriage checking papers, of which I had none, I asked a lady to help me. She took me to the lavatory with her. As the control neared the area, she opened the door and stepped into the corridor. I remained hidden inside."

16. ACT IT OUT

An escaper was hiding in France. A woman gave him some older farmer's clothes and a ticket for the train. She also wrote a note saying he was deaf, dumb, and mentally deficient and asked people to help him. "I slept that night in the waiting room with German soldiers. In the morning, two French policemen asked for my papers. Looking vacant, I gave them the note. After looking at it for a few seconds, they handed it back to me and let me pass."

17. WATCH FOR OPPORTUNITY

An evader watched the ticket window until there was a queue. He then joined in, on the theory that a busy railway ticket seller would not have time to be suspicious and ask questions. The advice is, "When buying a ticket, pick a busy time and say nothing except the destination."[4]

Finally Winfrey had actual stories of escape and evasion exploits—true accounts for his briefers to pass on, rather than fabrications and theories. Eager to get this information into Churchill's hands and put it to work, he hurried from his office to the Creamery across the street. It had indeed been a good day.

9

— ✕ —— ✕ —

THE ESCAPES OF "SHORTY" LEE GORDON

TOWARD THE END OF November 1943, MI-9's radio communication center in London received a signal from an MI-9 agent at Saint-Nicholas, France, by the name of Sergeant Major Lucien Dumais. Dumais, a Canadian, was in France on orders of MI-9 to set up the Shelburn Underground Escape Line and was requesting confirmation of a serviceman's identity: "Shorty" Lee Gordon had arrived in France claiming that he was an American airman escapee from Stalag VII-A at Moosburg, Germany.

MI-9 called Spaatz's Eighth Air Force headquarters, who verified Gordon's identity, radioed a confirmation to Dumais, and then arranged for a secret evacuation of the POW. Four days later, "Shorty" Lee Gordon was being debriefed in Stull Holt's office, and on December 3, Winfrey received a full report on America's first successful escapee.

The nickname "Shorty" came easily to Lee Gordon, as he stood but 5 feet, 2 inches. A daring hot-rod racer in his native California, he had tried to enlist in the Royal Canadian Air Force in 1940 but was rejected because of his size. As the war clouds darkened that same year, Shorty knew that the U.S. Army Air Force would be looking for small-framed men to be turret gunners. Once again attempting military enlistment, he was accepted this time in the 365th Bomb Squadron, 305th Bomb Group, which was among the first to arrive in England following the attack on Pearl Harbor.

Shorty was on his thirteenth bombing mission on February 26, 1943, as part of a mission of twenty bombers attacking Bremen, Germany. Fifty miles from the target, two Me-109 German fighters attacked, knocking out the number four engine. Flak tore up the right wing and wounded the tail gunner, Sergeant Lawrence C. Lovos. A second concentration of flak severely peppered the ship, killing Lieutenant Thomas D. Finlay, bombardier, and Staff Sergeant Peter Kekseo, top turret gunner. The pilot, Lieutenant George E. Stallman, ordered the rest of the crew to bail out.

Shorty rolled out of his turret and opened his chute at twenty-four thousand feet, nearly slipping through the harness because of his small frame. He landed, without incident, near a dyke, where a young girl was standing nearby. After shedding his parachute, he walked over to her and inquired where he was, in English. She responded in Dutch, and Shorty assumed that he was either in or close to Holland.

While he was talking to the girl, a very old German soldier rode up on a bicycle and took Shorty prisoner. Shorty was searched for weapons, but the search was cursory, and the German missed Shorty's escape kit and purse, which were in the leg pocket of his trousers. He was then marched to a nearby German flak post, where the German gunner showed Shorty a silhouette of a B-17 Flying Fortress and, pointing animatedly to it, said, "Ja, ja."

Later, toward evening, ten more men and two officers from Shorty's squadron were brought in, and the

Germans loaded them on a train for the Dulag Luft at Frankfurt. There, he was strip-searched, his escape kit, maps, and money purse confiscated, and his secret hide-out compass and gigili saw were discovered.

After four weeks in the Dulag, Shorty and seventeen other enlisted American airmen were issued British uniforms, as no U.S. uniforms were available, and were then marched under guard to the rail depot, where they were loaded in second-class carriages. A total of 118 British and American POWs were in the two carriages in the middle of a freight train. It was a four-day ride to Stalag VIII-B at Lamsdorf, one of the largest camps for British POWs. Upon arrival, the prisoners were fingerprinted, photographed, and issued a zinc identity dish with a POW number. Shorty's number was 27680.

At the camp, the British POWs had to wear handcuffs, owing to a recent but unsuccessful mass escape attempt, while three Americans captured at Dieppe walked about uncuffed.

After a week at Lamsdorf, all the American POWs were told to prepare for a transfer to an American camp. Forty men were subsequently loaded into a freight car, the door latch of which was secured by a piece of barbed wire. Shorty and seven other men banded together for an escape attempt, reasoning that an escape from the train would be much easier than one from a wire-enclosed camp.

Working at a small hole in the door, the group enlarged it sufficiently to allow a man to reach the wire on the locking latch. Near Chemnitz (Karl-Marx-Stadt today), as night fell and the train was slowing in its approach toward a long upgrade, the men decided to make a break. The door was opened, and three of them jumped. They anxiously looked ahead at the front car containing the guards, but there was no alarm. Three more men jumped, and still there was no alarm. Next, Sergeant Bernard Saltz and Shorty jumped. After Shorty hit the ground, he heard a human whistle and moved cautiously through the darkness toward it until he came upon Saltz. They sat quietly together, watching the lights of the train disappear into the night.

They left the area and climbed a small hill, where they rested until daylight so they could get their bearings. When they awoke, they saw a village and rail tracks ahead of them. Because they had previously decided to try to hop a freight train, they began to walk toward the town. As they drew close, they realized that there were too many people around who would see them board a train, so they walked through the village until they came upon an old man. Saltz, who could speak a little German, asked for a dish of water, which the man fetched. They thanked the man and moved on.

Rounding a turn in the road, they came upon a group of German soldiers walking toward them. Passing within five feet, the Germans paid no attention to Shorty and Saltz, even though they were still wearing their British overcoats and hats. Evidently these soldiers were not combat seasoned, or they surely would have recognized the uniform of their enemy.

Shorty and Saltz continued their trek through three more villages, passing at least one hundred people, all of whom took no notice of them.

After about ten kilometers (twenty-two miles), Shorty and Saltz once again saw railroad tracks and a village ahead of them. Skirting the village, they set a course for the tracks, but before they had gone a couple of hundred yards, police on bicycles and motorcycles surrounded them. After a quick search for weapons, Shorty and Saltz were taken in sidecars to the town jail.

Three days later, a German soldier took them on a train to Moosburg, where, arriving just before dark at Stalag VII-A, they were searched and admitted to the detention barracks.

The camp was filled with French, Russian, English,

Australian, and Canadian POWs who had previously escaped and been recaptured. Shorty and Saltz wanted to learn all they could about escapes and listened attentively as stories were told about methods of getting free, where and how recaptures occurred, why destinations were chosen, and difficulties experienced with patrols, fences, and dogs.

Shorty then began to plan his next escape and contacted escape committee member Technical Sergeant Kenneth Kurtenbach for help. Together they reviewed Shorty's previous escape attempt, studying the weak links in it that resulted in failure.

"We know from prior experiences that once you are out of the camp," Kurtenbach told Shorty, "you must travel fast to get out of the immediate area before the alarm is sounded. Know where you want to go and keep moving. Never stop to look at a map where people can see you. Anyone can ride slow trains for short distances without a permit, but buying a ticket can be a problem if you don't speak German."

Kurtenbach then paused and looked straight at Shorty. "What you need," he then said, "is a plan or disguise that will let you blend in with the populace and allow you to move quickly over distances without papers."

Shorty nodded, his mind racing, wondering what such a plan or disguise could be.

"German roads," Kurtenbach continued, "are usually well marked and have good bicycle paths, but stay off the Autobahn and the military roads."

Then he smiled, and leaned back. "Now, kid," he said with a grin, "I can give you a few cans of coffee, some cigarettes, a good compass, and one thousand Reichmarks . . . maybe even a few D-chocolate bars. With that you ought to be able to tame a guard and get something that will put you on the road again, don't ya' think?"

Shorty stared at Kurtenbach, stunned. "Where'd the committee get all that stuff?"

Kurtenbach did not answer but just smiled and, shaking Shorty's hand, said, "Good luck."

Shorty took his supplies and followed Kurtenbach's instructions. He traded a can of coffee with a French POW for a map of the Swiss border. With another POW, he traded cigarettes for a map of southern Germany that depicted the area from Ulm to the Rhine River. Then he studied the maps until he knew every detail on them by heart.

Next, he decided that he would try to steal a bicycle and pedal his way to freedom. He also knew that other POWs had tried this method and had been caught, so he would have to remain unnoticed, somehow. Civilian clothes would not be enough, as he would have to have the proper ID papers. As his size and lack of facial hair had often led others to mistake him for a boy of sixteen or younger, Shorty decided that these otherwise embarrassing traits could now be put to his advantage. If he could present himself as a German boy, he would have the necessary disguise for his escape. All he needed to play the part was a pair of Bavarian lederhosen.

He continued trading off items from his coffee and cigarette cache, acquiring a pocketknife, compass, and civilian knapsack, while simultaneously keeping close company with a British soldier who had many contacts with the guards. Finally, he outlined his plan to the soldier, who gave him additional ideas for his escape and advised him to seek out a certain guard who had a penchant for coffee and bribe him for the needed clothing. When Shorty received his next Red Cross food parcel, he raffled it off along with the northern half of his map for twenty cans of coffee, most of which he gave to the guard.

Three days later he received a pair of well-fitting lederhosen and a shirt, black jacket, and Innsbrucker hat. A Frenchman cut down Shorty's GI shoes to resemble civilian low-cuts, and the camp barber gave him a short, German-style haircut. Shorty then bribed a German guard for five hundred francs to obtain a bicycle and hide it a mile from the camp, where Shorty knew a work party went out daily from the camp.

On June 1, 1943, he donned his leather britches, covering them with his uniform. He volunteered for the work party of eighteen men and marched out of the camp under guard. As they neared his escape area, he watched for his chance and with three steps left the column to hide behind a large tree. Within five minutes he heard the Germans yelling and knew his absence had been discovered. Putting distance between himself and the road, he came upon a large field of oats, in which he laid down to rest and wait. Just before dark, he heard the search party called off, and he went back to the area where his bicycle was hidden.

He found the bribed guard waiting for him with a pair of worn civilian trousers and a coat. Shorty discarded his uniform and put on the civilian clothes, mounted the bicycle, and rode off. When he was ten kilometers (about six miles) from Munich, he stripped off his civilian clothes and assumed the appearance of a German boy, wearing lederhosen and pedaling merrily along on his bicycle. Passing numerous people, he always dutifully raised his right arm and loudly sang out "Heil Hitler," receiving a similar greeting from the civilians, policemen, and soldiers.

All went well until he neared Ulm, about 60 kilometers (37 miles) west of Munich, where it started to rain. He pulled off the road under a large tree and, placing his bicycle against one side of the trunk, went around to the other side, sat down, and was soon lost in a deep sleep. The sound of nearby voices woke him, and as he opened his eyes, he saw two German civilians holding his bicycle, addressing him. He was too deficient in German to be able to reply satisfactorily, and he was immediately taken to the town jail, where a search revealed his POW identity dish, resulting in a telephone call to the prison camp.

One week later, Shorty was back in Stalag VII-A at Moosburg, where he was placed in solitary for two weeks while the camp officials unsuccessfully interrogated him to learn the details of his escape. Shorty was then returned to the general population of POWs, where his friends and even the bribed German guard were happy to see him.

On July 3, Shorty began planning his third escape, which he decided would be through France this time instead of Switzerland. But before he could start his plans, the camp officials made a surprise search of the camp, which netted a large number of maps, compasses, forbidden books, wire, pliers, picks, shovels, chisels, hammers, hacksaws, money, and civilian clothes. Though this affected Shorty's acquisition of escape aids, it did not dampen his determination to escape again.

The opportunity came when word went through the camp that all American airmen would be moved to Stalag 17-B at Krems, Austria. Shorty changed identities with an Australian, Lloyd Ferguson, who also gave Shorty a complete set of civilian clothes. A French POW friend then introduced Shorty to a British army captain who also wanted to escape. As the captain spoke French, Shorty welcomed this colleague.

On October 13 Shorty received several packs of cigarettes and another one thousand Reichmarks from the escape committee. He packed his meager escape kit and arranged for an Australian to throw it over the enlisted men's fence into the officers' compound. With his cigarettes, Shorty was then able to bribe a guard to let him pass into the officers' compound, where he collected his kit and went to meet his escape companion, Captain Carr.

proceed to Post Office Box 1142, Alexandria, Virginia and [after] arrival there-at, report to the Commanding Officer by telephone Temple 8141."

On February 8, 1944, Lloyd Shoemaker, dressed in new green fatigues, reported to Major Winfrey at the Warehouse. After extending a warm welcome, Winfrey took him through the security door to the working area where he introduced him to Corporal Carl Peterson and instructed the corporal to fill the new man in on the operation.

Peterson was a quiet, easygoing individual, not particularly adapted to the army. His strong religious beliefs were reinforced by high moral standards, and he was a man capable of making a friend in a matter of minutes. With a knowing smile, he took obvious great delight in unfolding the secrets of MIS-X to Shoemaker. In a soft Rhode Island accent, he said, "Let's walk through the building, meet the crew, see the sights, and form your questions. Then we can talk."

They passed among the eight ten-foot-high shelves crammed with enough merchandise to make both J. C. Penney and A&P envious. In the far rear, Private First Class Maurice Hitchcock stopped his press long enough to display the counterfeit travel permits he was printing. A large German-English dictionary lay open on his workbench, adjacent to several slugs of German type. It was apparent to Shoemaker, who in his youth had worked in a print shop, that Hitchcock had been comparing the Gothic typeface of the permits to illustrations in the dictionary.

Peterson then took Shoemaker to the shop wing of the building, introducing him to the supervisor, Sergeant Bill Harris, and the crew, who was busy cutting, sanding, and gluing shaving and shoe brushes.

Corporal Peterson stopped by a workbench where Private First Class George Meidlein was busy cutting off the top of a shoe brush, held in a wood vice with hard rubber grips. Meidlein explained, "The rubber grips prevent the vice from scratching or leaving marks on the brush. The saw I am using is a surgical 'gigili' used by doctors to cut through a skull. It is chrome with molybdenum and tungsten additives for special hardening. It has very fine teeth, yet will cut through a steel bar in minutes. If we used a regular hacksaw, even with the finest teeth, the wooden edges of the brush would splinter and show up when it is glued back in place."

Meidlein then showed Shoemaker the shoe brush Private George E. Allen had in an adjacent vice, on which a router had been used to create a cavity. "We pack maps, money, or other papers in the cavity," Allen explained. "We can put five small maps or two large ones in. The top is put back using the special iron glue the Army Chemical Corps made for us. You can drop it, hit it, and it won't split open. You have to smash the brush to get at the contents."

On a corner table where Private First Class Sam Rubin was working, Peterson pointed to a steamer. "They steam apart the top layer of a Monopoly game board, then cut out a center cavity just like the shoe brush. Again, maps, money, or counterfeit papers are folded in and the top replaced."

Rubin volunteered, "We do the same with a checkerboard, the face of a Ping-Pong paddle, or many other games made with flat, layered paper. One of the best tricks is using a deck of playing cards. They cut a map into squares equal to a playing card. A square of map is placed between the laminated sections of a card. When all fifty-four cards are taken apart, the fifty-four map squares make one large map."

Shoemaker and Peterson then passed on to the longest workbench in the shop. Lieutenant James H.

McTighe was soldering terminals inside a hollowed-out cribbage board. He stopped long enough to explain that the board carried a crystal radio. Nails would be used instead of wooden matches to keep score, as the nails provided contact points for the radio. The batteries were specially made by Mallory for long life, and a hearing aid was used as an earphone.

Lieutenant Henry Brock sat at a desk where inventory was maintained. He explained that all contraband was marked "in" and "out" on very carefully kept records. Once an object was loaded, a small, round, gummed sticker was applied to it. The sticker was coded to identify what and how much was concealed inside the item. When the item was packed inside a parcel for shipment, the gummed label was removed, inventory levels were appropriately changed, and the sticker was transferred to a record that identified the name, address, and date of the shipment.

Peterson then explained to Shoemaker that MIS-X used two fictitious societies for its mailings. "The Servicemen's Relief and the War Prisoner's Benefit Foundation each have three different types of parcels: food, recreational, and clothing. But the food boxes are humanitarian and are never used to conceal escape aids. Each clothing parcel is somewhat different, but generally contain uniform shirts, trousers, field jackets, socks, and shoes. Sometimes a blanket, sheet, or half soles and heels served as substitutes."

Shoemaker gave Peterson a curious look.

"Using a razor blade," Peterson smiled, "the POWs can carve the latest official stamp from a rubber heel."

He then went on to explain that the recreation parcels consisted entirely of athletic or game materials, which were the major carriers for hidden aids. Each society had to use different brands of the same products and packaging materials, complete to wrapping paper and twine. Because the clothing was military uniforms, these alone could be the same between societies. Nothing was left to memory, from packing to dispatching a parcel. Every step was governed by a written outline and a checkoff list. On Winfrey's order, rigidly enforced, two men, with a checkoff list, packed and wrapped each parcel.

Peterson completed the indoctrination and pointed to the forty-five parcels on the counter, packed and ready to be sealed. Picking up a label, he pointed to the War Prisoner's Benefit Foundation across the top, and stated that they were recreation parcels destined for Stalag 17-B at Krems, Austria. A coded letter had been mailed the previous week, alerting the escape committee there of the names of the recipients of the "hot" parcels.

About two hours later, Winfrey summoned Shoemaker to the front office and instructed him to change into a class "A" uniform. Shoemaker was to go into Washington and purchase a dozen cans of flea and lice powder. The major gave him money and instructed him to obtain a cash receipt for the purchases. Winfrey reminded Shoemaker that the work, and even the base itself, were secret, and in the event of questioning by citizens, he was to use his own judgment in answering, keeping security in mind at all times. The instructions seemed simple enough, and Shoemaker drove off to the city to complete his errand.

He found a pharmacy at 14th and E streets, where several customers were waiting in line. When Shoemaker's turn came up, he told the pharmacist in a voice louder than he had intended "I need twelve cans of flea and lice powder, please."

The pharmacist blinked twice, smiled, and then questioned: "Twelve cans of lice powder?"

"Yes, sir."

"You actually want twelve cans of lice powder!"

By now the soldier was aware that all eyes were upon him, and a woman standing next to him suddenly moved away, as if standing too close to a hot stove. Self-consciously, Shoemaker looked back at the pharmacist and, in a voice now barely audible, answered "Yes, please. Twelve cans of flea and lice powder."

The pharmacist went off to the rear of the store, returning in a few moments with a medium-sized grocery bag loaded with the order. As Shoemaker received his cash receipt and was turning to leave, the pharmacist asked him, "Where are you stationed, soldier?"

Being new to the area, the only military base Shoemaker could think of was Fort Myer, home of the General Staff. "Fort Myer," Shoemaker called out and went quickly through the door.

The next morning, while Shoemaker was helping Peterson in the Warehouse, Winfrey entered, carrying a newspaper. Stopping in front of Shoemaker, Winfrey asked if there had been any problems while on his errand. Shoemaker replied in the negative just as the major slapped the newspaper on the counter. It had been folded to reveal an article written by a young columnist in Washington. The banner line read "GENERAL STAFF LOUSY—G.I.'S BUY LICE POWDER."

Just before noon the next day, Shoemaker returned from town wearing his new government-financed civilian togs!

Two days later, the motor pool sergeant at 1142 brought a 1940 Dodge panel truck up to the Warehouse in the morning and parked it, giving the keys to Corporal Huss. Per Winfrey's instructions, the vehicle was coal black, with no identifying insignia to indicate that it was a military vehicle, and the new tires—even the spare— were exchanged for five worn "bologna skins." Civilian license plates had been secured from Washington, with the registration file holding a notation that all inquiries as to ownership were to be referred to the commissioner of vehicles in Washington, D.C.

Upon being notified that the vehicle had arrived, Winfrey called Shoemaker and the two of them inspected the truck. Winfrey told Shoemaker that the vehicle must appear to be civilian at all times and was never to depart 1142 with less than a full tank of gas. In any emergency, Shoemaker was to extricate himself using his own ingenuity. Otherwise, he was to phone Major T. M. Harris in Colonel Johnston's office at the Pentagon for assistance. Winfrey then had Shoemaker memorize Harris's phone number.

While Peterson and Shoemaker loaded the truck with nine mailbags containing the forty-five parcels for Stalag 17-B, Winfrey went inside and changed into civilian clothing. Winfrey and Shoemaker, both wearing mufti, then drove to the post office in Baltimore, where Winfrey showed Shoemaker how to obtain a postal cart by ringing a bell that summoned the mail clerk. By the time the mail sacks had been loaded onto the cart, the supervisor appeared and wheeled the cart to the far corner of the sorting room.

Winfrey explained to Shoemaker that the supervisor would read the coded routing tag and place the parcels into the mail system.

They then drove to the Ben Franklin store in Baltimore, where Winfrey told Shoemaker that the War Prisoner's Benefit Foundation and the Servicemen's Relief both had open accounts with the store as well as contracts for the store to receive and hold drop shipments for merchandise purchased elsewhere. Winfrey introduced Shoemaker to the store manager as an employee of the two societies, indicating that their business was to supply U.S. prisoners of war. The manager eagerly welcomed them without question, though an eyebrow was raised when Shoemaker signed for a small box containing one dozen pairs of nylon hosiery, which, Winfrey later explained, the POWs used to bribe German guards for assistance in carrying contraband into the camps.

As they returned to 1142 that afternoon, Winfrey looked at Shoemaker and said, "Well, that's generally how things should go. You'll be in civilian clothes from here on out. Get used to being thought of as 4-F."

11

—✗———✗—

TUNNELING

DURING THE SECOND WEEK of March 1944, Major Leo H. Crosson reported to 1142 as Winfrey's executive officer. A chemical engineer, Crosson was from the old South, with a soft drawl that was a delight to the ear, yet so thick that "Ya'al damn Yankees" often required a repeat. Being good natured, he readily took to the unmilitary atmosphere of 1142 and was quickly appreciated by the technical and correspondence sections as a capable and efficient addition to the staff.

The major was totally awed by the operation of MIS-X as Winfrey briefed him while walking through the Warehouse. The orientation ended in the Creamery, where Winfrey suggested Crosson spend the remainder of the day with the technicians to satisfy his curiosity about the operation. Before separating, Winfrey told Crosson, "Leo, I suggest you get our show down pat because I'm off to the air corps headquarters to meet with their staff and ask for an operational appropriation. When I return, in about a week, it'll be your turn to meet with the ground forces."

Crosson displayed a sincere interest in the MIS-X

mission and adopted Winfrey's habit of arriving at the Warehouse early in the morning and remaining until late in the evening.

On March 25 Winfrey returned successfully with a $25,000 grant. Major Crosson felt equal to approaching the army ground forces staff for more operational funds, and on March 26 departed for the infantry headquarters at Fort Benning, Georgia.

At about this time, a mysterious donation of $1 million was also deposited into Winfrey's secret MIS-X account. Though never proven, it was suspected that this money came from the generosity of Colonel Johnston in the Pentagon.

With the unit financially solvent again, Winfrey told Shoemaker to forage through all the grocery stores along his route to the Baltimore post office for staples. Dried food such as beans, apricots, apples, prunes, and raisins were to be purchased wherever they could be found, even if it meant clearing a shelf in a store. Items such as coffee, tea, sugar, canned milk, chewing gum, and cigarettes were being purchased directly from the manufacturers by the humanitarian societies, and Shoemaker was instructed to pass by these items.

The next day, March 27, as Shoemaker prepared for his run, he reported to Corporal Huss in Winfrey's office and received $200 in small bills. Huss had a typed receipt ready for Shoemaker's signature, together with a receipt book that all vendors had to sign.

Dressed in civilian clothes, money in hand Shoemaker headed north on U.S. Highway 1. At College Park, Maryland, Shoemaker located several boxes of assorted dried fruits in a store and proceeded to empty the shelf. At the checkout counter, the clerk glared at Shoemaker but made no comment. However, a woman in line behind Shoemaker became very irate upon seeing the size of the purchase. "Hoarder!" she screamed, and smashed a tomato on his shoulder.

In a Baltimore drugstore, Shoemaker discovered seven bottles of malted milk tablets, an item very much desired by POWs. But at the checkout stand, the druggist denied the sale, allowing Shoemaker only one bottle. "They are for my brother, who is a POW," Shoemaker pleaded. In an unsympathetic tone, the druggist said "You sure as hell look fit enough. Why aren't you in uniform—you could take them to him!"

Late that afternoon, Shoemaker returned to the Warehouse and surrendered the purchases to Corporal Peterson, who entered them on his inventory cards. The receipt book and cash change went to Corporal Huss, who determined that the tally was correct.

But as MIS-X was beginning to renew its optimism and productivity, events were taking place in Europe that would profoundly affect its operations.

On March 25, just after 4:00 A.M., a guard was patrolling the north side of Stalag Luft III's North Compound when he saw a form in the semidarkness. At first he thought it was a fellow guard from the east fence who had extended his patrol in order to visit. But as the form approached and became clearer, the guard saw instead a man standing before him with his hands raised. The guard's thumb snapped off the rifle safety, and he took a step forward. Then two more men suddenly appeared from behind a bush, and they too had their hands raised in a sign of surrender.

During this entire time, the guard had not spoken a single word, as he had been taken by complete surprise. Now events were becoming further complicated, as a fourth man emerged from a previously unnoticed hole in the ground nearby where the three surrendering men stood. The guard suddenly raised his rifle into the air and fired a shot, ordering the four men before him to remain motionless. He realized that he had stumbled upon an escape attempt.

Within seconds, more German soldiers arrived from

the guardhouse three hundred feet away. Carrying flash-lights, the soldiers shined the lights into the darkness and saw before them men dressed in what appeared to be civilian clothes. A two-foot-square hole in the ground behind these men gave evidence of how they had gotten to this side of the camp's wire.

Detailing two men to remain at the hole in order to prevent further escapes, the guards herded their four captives to the camp's headquarters, where Colonel Friedrich-Wilhelm von Lindeiner, camp commandant, and his staff were now quickly assembling.

One week later, on April 1, Colonel Johnston arrived at the Warehouse. Having been alerted to the visit, Huss had the Warehouse door open as the staff car stopped in front of the building. Major Winfrey was at the entry as Johnston climbed the steps.

"Congratulations, Robbie," were Johnston's first words. "You have been promoted to Lieutenant Colonel."

Winfrey, obviously pleased, said, "Thank you, Colonel," and exhibited one of his rare smiles.

But as they walked into the office area, Winfrey could tell that Johnston was in no mood for levity. Johnston declined the offer of a chair, stating, "I'd like to address all personnel of both sections in the briefers' room."

Winfrey now grew concerned about Johnston's somber tone and nodded to Huss, who already had his hand on the telephone to call the Creamery.

It took but five minutes for the combined personnel to assemble at one end of the briefers' room, with Johnston and Winfrey at the opposite end. Colonel Johnston began: "Men, I have some bad news, and like all bad news it travels fast. For the past five months you have done one hell of a good job dispatching escape aids to the American POWs at Stalag Luft III. From the tone of messages we've received—and other means of communication—we have suspected something big was in the making in North Compound. And indeed it was.

"For the past seven months, the combined nationalities in North Compound have been digging three very long tunnels. They named them 'Tom,' 'Dick,' and 'Harry.' They were twenty-six feet deep, too deep for the Germans to locate with probe rods, and Tom and Dick were each over two hundred feet long.

"During the night of March 24, seventy-six POWs made their way 335 feet through Harry to escape."

Smiles broke out on the faces of the men who stood listening to Johnston. Some began punching one another on the shoulder as a feeling of pride overcame them.

"Wait!" Johnston said above the noise. "There's more. As you all know, Germany is a strong police state, making it very difficult for a POW to move about once he gets past the wire. I deeply regret to advise you that of the seventy-six men who passed through that tunnel, all but three have been recaptured. But worse, Hitler ordered fifty shot in cold blood, and we understand that the Gestapo has obliged."

There was total silence in the room for a full minute. Then Johnston continued.

"Twenty-three have been returned to Stalag Luft III's North Compound. We have no word on the remaining three men. Brigadier Crockatt will phone additional details as soon as they can be determined. This tragic story will not be released to the press for another seventy-two hours, as the British are waiting for a list of names so they can first notify the next of kin."

"Were there any American POWs involved?" Winfrey asked in a soft voice.

"No. Nearly all the Americans had been moved to South Compound eight weeks prior, where they are under Colonel Charles Goodrich's command."

The room remained silent, and there was very little

movement even after Winfrey said "Dismissed, gentlemen."

THE STORY OF THIS heroic but tragic effort has been told numerous times in film and book. It has been referred to as the Great Escape, but the full story has never been told. It is as follows:

Tunnels Tom, Dick, and Harry each originated inside a barracks, in preparation for a mass escape that was projected to include two hundred POWs. All tunnels were to be thirty feet deep, whereas prior tunnels had not exceeded ten feet. While all three tunnels were well over two hundred feet each, Harry, the escape tunnel, was 336 feet long. The diggers moved and hid 160 tons of sand in their excavation, requiring two hundred "penguins" to carry and spread the sand in the compound. Squadron Leader Wally Floody, a Canadian mining engineer, was in charge, directing the diggers while other POWs in "factories" were busy converting blankets and military uniforms into civilian clothes. The forgery department was creating all types of IDs, and mappers were tracing maps using indelible lead.

Lieutenant Colonel Albert Clark, as camp security officer, or "Big S," divided North Compound into two sections, with that portion nearest the gate being the S, or safety, zone, and the remainder being the D, or danger, zone. Whenever a roving ferret penetrated into D zone, he would be followed by a stooge and warnings were relayed to the projects. If a German appeared too near a working area, he would be encountered by a stooge, who would detain him for the few seconds it took the workers to cover up their projects. All total, there were six hundred stooges employed as lookouts, none of whom ever knew precisely what they were guarding.[1]

Clothing for the escape was made from bed sheets, blankets, uniforms of various nationalities, towels, pieces of kit bags, and from clandestine shipments from MI-9 and MIS-X. Dyes were made from indelible leads, permanganate of potash, gentian violet stolen from sick bay, coffee or tea, boiled book bindings, or by actually trading for dyes with a "tame" guard. All dyeing was done in the barracks at night, and each article had to be dry before morning roll call.[2]

About fifty sets of blue coveralls were made, similar to those worn by the German ferrets. Forty-two German uniforms with caps, belts, and buckles were made, with the insignia and buttons produced from molten lead foil taken from cigarette packs poured into molds of soap or plaster casts stolen from the hospital. Belts were made from black tar paper taken from barracks walls or made by altering leather boots. Two hundred and sixty civilian jackets were made by removing the pockets and belts from uniform tunics and rounding off the sharp corners of the collars. Two hundred and thirty pairs of civilian trousers were made from dyed uniforms or from scraping wool blankets with a razor to resemble serge. One hundred civilian suits were converted from uniforms. Three hundred civilian caps were converted from uniforms or made from cardboard. Travel permits, work permits, ration coupons, personal IDs, discharge papers, pay books, leave papers, and even passports were counterfeited. All were hand-drawn and forged with colored stamps, hand-carved from a rubber shoe heel. Many documents, hand-lettered to resemble typing, took a month to complete but passed numerous inspections by the Gestapo.[3]

Those digging the tunnels, other than the British, were French, Poles, Belgians, Dutch, and Americans. Among the Americans involved in digging all three tunnels was Major David M. "Tokyo" Jones, who had been on General Jimmy Doolittle's Japanese raids. His dramatic firsthand account gives an intimate view of this incredible feat:

I ended up in East Compound with Lieutenant Colonel Clark. My birthday was December 18, the day I entered the camp. Colonel Clark was senior officer at that time, so I reported to him, and he put me to work. The first job he gave me was to move a wall in the barracks, so we could find places to hide incoming contraband. That was my introduction to escape activities.

At that point in time, the British had pretty well made their plans for the three tunnels, so we all went to work in the various areas. Memories are still quite vivid. I guess sometimes when we were thirty feet under and it was time to come out and get counted, and the sand fell in on us, we wondered, "What the hell am I doing here?" But, at any rate, it was a great time, and very satisfying because there were just a few of us, and I was one Yank in the middle of several thousand British, and I had to hold up my end.

Well, I recall the first day I went to work with Squadron Leader Wally Floody. We were going down what I believe was Tom, and we were down about thirty feet, and maybe fifty feet back in the tunnel, when the lamp kept going out. It was a homemade lamp, fired by fat or margarine, and we used a pajama string for a wick. So I sent the lamp back up to be lit, and when it came down it went out again. This went on for quite a while, until we realized there was not enough oxygen in the hole to support that tiny flame. That sort of set the tone for our work.

Another thing . . . we wore longjohns, one-piece wool underwear type things. We had to wear them because the sand stained us. It was wet and damp. When we got that deep, the sand had a lot of clay in it, which was different colored than the surface sand. So we got stained and just couldn't take a chance on showing different colors that came up from the hole. It was a horrible experience to pull on a pair of those wet, clammy longjohns and climb down in that dark hole to go to work. But that is the way it was.

We dug pretty much as a team. Buck [Ingram] and I dug a lot together. We got pretty far with that tunnel. There wasn't enough room to turn around in the tunnel, so after 100 feet, we made a place called "Grand Central Station." It was just a space dug out of the tunnel walls, a wide spot. I'm 6'2" and just too tall to curl around like the other fellows who worked down there. It was dark . . . we were always "feeling" our moves. We had to shore the walls and ceiling all the way with the bed boards. You know, we slept on bed boards in the barracks—and each guy would give up two or three boards which we used. By the time we collected them all, we had three thousand. But remember, we were digging *three* long tunnels.

Then we would come to a stretch which we thought would hold, and just put a few boards in the top of the tunnel. Then we'd have a cave-in, and the guy working got buried, and the man behind would have to dig him out—always in the dark. It was a hairy situation, but we realized we just couldn't quit—there were so many thousands of people behind us that were counting on our job to get done. So many thousands of man-hours into this thing. No matter how scared, we just could not leave the job. We had to—even if we were covered up and they dug us out—we had to go right back in there again and start digging.

. . . Then, eight weeks before the big escape, we [the Americans] were moved to South Compound. At first it was heartbreaking to leave.

Most of us, I'm sure, would have qualified to be near the head of the list to go out once it was done. But we would have to go out "hard-ass," you know, most of us did not speak German. We didn't have any special qualification, which is the way you really line up such things. But the guy that had a chance to get out and get home was the guy who could speak the language and not have to go "hard-ass."[4]

Unfortunately, most of those recaptured after the Great Escape could also not speak German and had to go "hard-ass." Their inability to pass as Germans caused their failure and ultimately their deaths.

The story of the Great Escape worked its way through the POW camps and temporarily halted escape activities. But what Major David Jones said of those involved in the Great Escape was true of every POW everywhere: "No matter how scared, we just could not leave the job," and soon escape activities were resumed in the camps with even greater determination and tenacity.

MIS-X, likewise momentarily stunned by the tragedy of the Great Escape, renewed its efforts with even greater boldness than before. A million and a half German forces drawn from the ranks of the Hitler Youth, Landwache, civilian police, and armed forces had been tied up in the apprehension of the escapees.

The war behind the barbed wire was having its effect, and Winfrey intended to push it to the limits.

The author and unmarked MIS-X truck outside of Warehouse. *(Author's collection)*

Master Sergeant Silvio A. Bedini, MIS-X cryptoanalyst (left), with author. *(Author's collection)*

General John K. Waters, Commander in Chief, U.S. Army, Pacific (ret.), was a lieutenant colonel at Oflag 64, and a code user. *(Author's collection)*

Lieutenant General Albert P. Clark, Jr., "Big S" at Stalag Luft III. *(USAFA Library)*

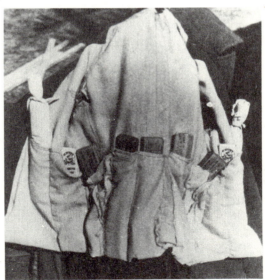

Escape vest made by POWs, designed to be worn under a coat. The pockets hold "D" ration chocolate, malt tablets, and canned milk sent by MIS-X. *(USAFA Library)*

Stalag Luft III, Sagan, Germany, an air officers' POW camp. *(Smithsonian Archives)*

Tunnel-digging crew at Stalag Luft III. Major David M. Jones is second from left. *(USAFA Library)*

12

---×———×———

RADIO COMES
TO BASEBALL

In mid-April 1944, Winfrey received a letter from Brig-adier Norman Crockatt that outlined how MI-9 had overcome the time-consuming difficulties of individually loading aids into carriers. "A simple solution," he wrote, "is to have the manufacturers do it."[1]

Winfrey liked the time-saving tip and after securing approval from Colonel Johnston, instructed Major Leo H. Crosson to extend his trips to include visits with the manufacturers of materials that were either used by or could be of use to MIS-X. Crosson then went on the road for two weeks to meet with various industrialists, but he was not always able to obtain the cooperation of the manufacturers he contacted, as MIS-X did not have the leverage of MI-9's governmental backing.

Under England's Official Secrets Act, a government official could swear an industrialist to secrecy regarding a national security matter and then compel his company to supply its wares or cooperate in some other way. In effect, therefore, MI-9 could force the nation's manufac-turers to assist in its activities. Major Clayton Hutton, a brilliant but vehemently independent member of MI-9, was able to use the Official Secrets Act to great advantage, obtaining numerous services and products from English industrialists that he then used for ingenious E&E devices that he personally created for MI-9. In addition to Hutton, Charles Fraser-Smith, a civilian in the clothing department of the Ministry of Supply, was adept at using the Official Secrets Act to aid the efforts of MI-9.[2]

The United States had no statutes similar to England's Official Secrets Act that Winfrey or Crosson could use as leverage, and thus they had to appeal to each manufacturer under the banner of patriotism. This approach was further complicated by the fact that Winfrey and Crosson could not reveal to the manufacturers the identity or activities of MIS-X. Their appeal had to be general and humanitarian.

When Crosson returned from this trip, Winfrey departed for a meeting with two executives of the F. W. Sickle Electronics Company at Chicopee, Massachusetts. He carried a diagram for a miniature radio transmitter that Lieutenant James H. McTighe had developed in the Warehouse. The transmitter required four basic parts, which POWs would not be able to obtain even with the utmost ingenuity.

Winfrey specified that, because the four parts of the transmitter were delicate, each had to be wrapped separately in cotton before being placed in a small aluminum capsule, which Sickle had on hand and was using for another purpose. The company was asked to make twelve sets of each part, and the capsules, forty-eight in all, were then to be shipped to the Goldsmith Baseball Company in Cincinnati, Ohio.

Sickle could and would make the four parts in the quantity Winfrey had requested, packaging them in capsules, wrapped in cotton. But shipping the forty-eight capsules to a baseball company brought raised eyebrows. The two executives were told only that it was a secret project for the war effort and no further explanations could be extended. After Winfrey pledged the two to secrecy, they affirmed that they, themselves, would remain after hours, wrap and conceal the parts, and package them for mailing.

When Winfrey returned to 1142, he called Shoemaker into the office and advised him that he was to leave for Cincinnati that night by rail. "You will arrive in the morning," Winfrey told him. "Get your business done and catch the night train back here. Wear civilian attire and if you have any problems, phone the Pentagon number for advice. Any questions?"

"No, sir, I understand," replied Shoemaker, as he accepted the expense money from Winfrey and signed a receipt for it.

When he arrived in Cincinnati, Shoemaker took a bus to within a block of the address Winfrey had given him. The baseball company was housed in a two-story stucco building nestled between two other buildings near the end of the street. A sign on the door read "Enter."

"Good morning," Shoemaker said, greeting the female clerk seated just inside the door. "My name is Shoemaker, and I have an appointment with Mr. Goldsmith."

Without looking up, the woman pointed with her pencil toward an open door behind her. A man's voice called out, "In here, Shoemaker. I'm Goldsmith."

The inner office Shoemaker entered was small, dusty, and littered with large advertising posters of baseball players. Goldsmith rose from behind a large, old desk that had clearly been abused by numerous cigarettes. Shaking Shoemaker's hand, Goldsmith pointed to a straight-backed chair, saying, "Get comfortable. Winfrey phoned me last week and said the government wanted some special baseballs wound. Why do I have to wind balls when I got a shelf full of them?"

"Well, sir," Shoemaker started slowly, "you'll be receiving four dozen small aluminum capsules. We'd like you to wind them as the core in four dozen special balls."

"Those balls won't sail true without the rubber core in the center," Goldsmith protested.

"They'll be fine, Mr. Goldsmith," Shoemaker said calmly, trying to assure him. "They will not be used to play ball. The government will substitute them for an expensive product used in secret experiments. Mr. Winfrey says your baseballs are the best made. This project is very important to the war effort, and Mr. Winfrey said that you are a man we can trust."

Sensing an unspoken meaning, Goldsmith said in a resigned tone, "I don't understand, but I'll do it."

Shoemaker told Goldsmith that each of the four dozen capsules would be marked with a spot of paint—twelve would be red, twelve green, twelve yellow, and twelve white. Great care must be taken to wind only one color at a time and to place a gummed label on the outside of the ball to denote the color of the capsule in the core. "Sounds okay to me," he said. "It isn't any more weird than what we're doing to the inside of the ball."

Shoemaker then told Goldsmith to send the finished balls to Mr. Robley Winfrey, in care of the Ben Franklin store in Baltimore, Maryland.

Forty-four years later, the author traced Goldsmith to a southern city. Goldsmith denied that he was the same "Mr. Goldsmith" being sought, saying, "I am not that person. I never did it. Besides, I promised the government I would never talk about it."[3]

One of these baseballs reached Stalag Luft III in the following way. It was during August 1944, an issuing day for Center Compound, as parcel officer for the three American camps, Captain Robert E. Williams was about to depart for the censoring office when he received word that one of his regular helpers was ill. There was little time to spare, as the Germans were quite punctual and an agitated censor could be difficult to work with. Williams went to Colonel Delmar T. Spivey's cubicle, as Spivey was Center Compound senior American officer and was responsible for assigning a new man to fill in. As the two men talked, Spivey noticed Captain Jack Oliver approaching and called out to him.

"Captain Oliver, I need you for a special job in the parcel office this morning. Williams has a man ill. Now listen closely, Jack, as I only have time to give you instructions once."

Oliver was not a member of the escape committee but had been in the camp since January 1943 and knew that there was a tight security policy. He suspected that he was about to become privy to something intriguing.

"Go along with Williams," Spivey told him, "and stay alert. Watch Williams and the crew and follow their cue. There is a softball coming through in one of the parcels. We don't want the censor looking at it too closely. It's damn important, Captain, that we get that ball into the camp." Oliver nodded his head and followed Williams to the censor office.

Oliver was working with the other men at the receiving table for about an hour when a box was opened and he saw a softball comfortably nestled in a bed of men's handkerchiefs. Quickly, he racked his brain for some way to get his hands on the ball, as POWs were not allowed to touch the contents of a package in front of the censor. The first thought that came to him was of the soft, gray texture of the cover of the ball, which he realized was horse hide.

He immediately began a conversation with the bored English-speaking guard standing next to him, inviting him to feel the soft skin of the ball. The guard did what Oliver hoped he would do and not only felt the ball but picked it up. Smiling as he felt it, the guard then passed it over to Oliver. Stepping back, Oliver gently tossed the ball back to the guard, who in turn took a step back and tossed it back to Oliver. Soon their game carried the guard to the door of the office, so he stepped outside where they could continue increasing the skill and distance of the game. When the guard's back was to the camp's fence, Oliver wound up and let fly a fastball that passed over the guard's head, over the fence, and into the compound. Some POWs who were standing by, idly watching Oliver and the guard, picked up the ball and began a game among themselves. An escape committee officer then came and took the ball away, and Center Compound had the fourth and final part of its much sought-after radio.[4]

WHILE SHOEMAKER WAS IN Cincinnati for the baseball project, Winfrey had also ordered him to visit the U.S. Playing Card Company. The company had been printing tissue paper maps for MIS-X, but the maps crinkled when concealed in the lining of a serviceman's jacket, and they disintegrated in the rain. Winfrey had called the general manager, advising him to cancel all future orders and await new instructions upon Shoemaker's arrival.

The playing card company was in a huge multistory red-brick structure in the industrial area of Cincinnati. Arriving by taxi, Shoemaker made his way into the lobby, and after giving his name to the receptionist, he was cleared to climb the wide, mahogany-lined stairwell, where the general manager, Matthew A. Follman, and the company engineer greeted him and showed him into the manager's office.

After a few minutes of polite talk, Shoemaker handed Follman a package containing several eighteen-by-twenty-eight-inch silk maps that had been sent to Winfrey by MI-9. They had been printed in four colors by the John Waddington Company of Leeds, England, which for many years had printed opera programs on silk for the royal family. Each of the different maps in fine detail illustrated a very small area of Germany, Poland, France, or Switzerland.

"Mr. Follman," Shoemaker told the general manager, "my mission is two-fold. First, I am to ask you if you will print, in silk and in the same colors, one hundred each of these fifty maps which we will supply you with. Also, I am to ask you to please add pectin to your inks, as this will cause them to coagulate and prevent them from running together."

Follman rocked back in his chair, as if considering the request. "It's an interesting idea," he finally said, "and just possibly practical. I believe we can accommodate you."

The engineer nodded in agreement.

"Now, gentlemen," Shoemaker continued, "you each have pledged your word on security to Mr. Winfrey, so I'm going to tell you the rest of our plans. Is it possible to take one of those small maps and cut it into fifty-six equal parts and sandwich each part between the two laminated pieces of a playing card? You would have to use the two jokers and the company logo cards to come out even, of course."

Both men's eyebrows shot up like runaway window blinds, and the silence lasted for several seconds.

"No," the engineer finally said, "the lamination process we use would not work. And the thickness of the map insert multiplied by fifty-six times would require a larger box—and I don't think you want to be conspicuous, do you?"

Then he added, before Shoemaker could respond, "You see, for a card player's security, the interiors of the cards are blackened so light can't penetrate to reveal the figures on the face."

"I know from meeting with Mr. Winfrey," Follman

continued, "that we are not to ask questions, but are you sure that this is what you want? It's most unusual."

"I'm sorry, gentlemen," Shoemaker said, sensing failure, "but it's important to get those maps into cards. Believe me, it's vital."

The engineer suddenly broke into a smile, and winking at the manager, he said, "Maps between layers of playing cards. Is that all you want?"

"Yes, sir," Shoemaker answered, sensing a renewed possibility of success. "Just put the map segments between the front and back portions of the cards."

Follman now came alive. Looking at his engineer, he exclaimed, "Are you thinking what I think you are thinking? Hell, yes! Take a block as we run it, eliminate the security black filament in the center . . . but how will they retrieve the maps?"

"I figure," the engineer said confidently, "a good rubber-base adhesive would separate without shattering, and the excess adhesive would rub off easily by just using one's thumb. That would leave a clean face on the map. How does that sound to you, Mr. Shoemaker?"

He then added quickly, "But before you answer, let me tell you what we can propose. We print, in a block, fifty-two cards, two jokers, and two company logo cards. Without going through the entire process, let's just print your map on the interior side of a block. We can work up a soft adhesive that will let the card be peeled easily. We will run the block through the cutter in the normal fashion, and we can put a pull-away gummed sticker on the boxes with a number to correspond to the map number inside the box. Now, Mr. Shoemaker, can you buy that?"

Shoemaker was thrilled that a solution had come up, but he was not authorized to sanction this change. "I'll convey your offer to Mr. Winfrey," he said, "and he will be in touch with you in the near future. Meanwhile, may

I advise him that you are proceeding with printing the silk maps?"

"Yes, indeed," said Follman, as the three rose, concluding their meeting.

When Winfrey heard the new plan, he approved the card company's suggestion, and several hundred decks were shipped into POW camps throughout 1944. The coded, numbered sticker on the box worked well, and the sealing stamp was placed just slightly off center, to alert camp committee members that this deck was "hot."

Forty-five years later, Ray F. Ostrander reported that he had been with the U.S. Playing Card Company since 1938. "After the country entered the war," Ostrander said, "I was the assistant controller, and was called in to help the president, Mr. Follman, and the engineer modify some of our machinery to print hydrographic charts for the navy. Then I donned a uniform and went off to war. The company was deeply involved in several aspects of secret war work at that time, and we learned not to ask too many questions."

Was he aware that the company printed silk maps?

"Well, yes," Ostrander replied. "We printed maps of areas in Europe on silk. But I never knew they were used for escape." He also recalled the details of the map transfer process. "We used apple pectin. It was a coagulant for the inks, as we were printing on both sides of silk."

Asked if he knew that the maps were inserted between the cards, Ostrander said, "I was fully aware. But later on, when I entered the army, I became involved with the OSS doing some secret work, and they told me again about the map segments in the cards. Having been sworn to secrecy when I worked for the company, I accepted the information as if it were new to me."[5]

*   *   *

WHILE SHOEMAKER AND CROSSON were acquiring manufacturer cooperation, Winfrey conceived of a unique way of providing POWs with compasses. He contacted the Gillette Razor Company in Boston and asked if they would magnetize their double-edged blades so that when a blade was balanced on a stick or held by a string, the *G* in the company trade name would point to the north. Winfrey also asked that the company conceal top-secret messages on the obverse side of each blade, which would appear when a POW rubbed off the trade writing on the blade. In addition, Winfrey asked if they would load maps and money into the hollow handles of the razors themselves. "Hot" boxes of blades would be identified by a faint lot number imprinted over the company name on the box. The lot number would also be the key to what the message said and enable MIS-X to correlate the shipment of each box to an appropriate POW camp. The Gillette executives agreed to stay after regular hours to perform the clandestine work personally. All total, five thousand magnetized blades were manufactured by Gillette and at least one thousand razor handles were loaded with escape materials.

Winfrey also contacted the Scoville Company in Waterbury, Connecticut, which manufactured the twenty-five million buttons used for army uniforms. Winfrey asked that they set aside five million of these buttons and place a compass inside each. A POW would twist the button counterclockwise to remove the concealed compass. When this trick was discovered by the Germans, "foxy Winfrey"—as many under the lieutenant colonel called him—ordered the screw reversed so that it opened clockwise, and every German thereafter, twisting one of the buttons during a search of a POW, only tightened it.

As a former executive at the R. J. Reynolds Company, Colonel Johnston requested hundreds of cartons of cigarettes, which were donated to MIS-X's two humanitarian societies. Lieutenant McTighe had designed a crystal radio receiver that fit inside a pack of cigarettes. MIS-X steamed off the stamp that sealed the pack, removed the cigarettes, and replaced them with the radio. The pack would then be resealed and returned to the carton from which it had come.

In the course of MIS-X activities, many other manufacturers were requested to assist in the surreptitious insertion of escape aids into their products. Most were surprised at such a request but, when pledged to secrecy, asked no further questions and admirably aided the nation's war effort. Without their time-saving service, it is doubtful the technical section of MIS-X could have maintained the pace set as the war escalated on the continent. The many companies not only geared their services to MIS-X's timetables but guarded their secret work through the years, often "forgetting" to enclose an invoice for their services. The U.S. Playing Card Company, the Gillette Razor Company, and the R. J. Reynolds Company, to name but a few, never billed for their services or products.

Production and shipping at MIS-X consequently increased and became more efficient; between 80 and 120 parcels a day were being sent to POWs throughout the European theater.

But the supply of German money to send to POWs, which MIS-X had been obtaining from American banks, was running low. Meanwhile, the Germans were printing phony British currency in an attempt to disrupt England's economy. Winfrey felt it was time for his group to balance the scales.

On a morning in the first week of May, the security door of the Warehouse flew open, and Winfrey bounded up to the long packaging counter where Peterson and Shoemaker were bagging parcels for the morning run. Calling for Hitchcock to leave his press and come forward, the colonel slowly unrolled a small cloth bundle on the counter, revealing two silver-colored metal plates. "Maurice," he said, addressing the printer, "you once said you could—now do it!"

Late that afternoon, when Shoemaker returned from Baltimore, he found Peterson and Hitchcock busy counting stacks of new Reichmarks, all counterfeit.

13

---x-------x---

"SEND
SMALL-CALIBER GUNS
FOR CLOSE SNIPING"

ON MAY 2, 1944, a coded letter from Oflag 64 was received by Master Sergeant Silvio Bedini at the
correspondence section of 1142. When decoded, the
message read: "Send small-caliber guns and ammo for
close sniping PD Message follows PD." Winfrey read
this message with great concern, as it suggested that
some critical project was being considered by the POWs.
Requesting guns and ammunition to be shipped to a
POW camp indicated that some form of drastic action
was being plotted by the prisoners. What was happening,
or was about to happen, inside the camp? Winfrey's
questions needed answers before he could comply with
the request.

MIS-X maintained detailed, up-to-date files on all
POW camps in Europe, and Winfrey asked his clerk,
Corporal Paul Huss, to bring him the Oflag 64 file. It
told him that Schubin, where Oflag 64 was located, was a
small market town 150 miles northwest of Warsaw, lying
in a plains area devoted primarily to agriculture. The
camp had been a girls' school before the Germans took it
over in 1940, converting it into a prison camp.

Consisting of several brick dormitories amid many large shade trees, the compound lay along a cobblestoned road, two miles from a rail depot. The camp originally held French and British POWs, until 1943, when Americans started arriving from the North African campaign. Colonel Thomas Drake was the senior American officer (SAO), having replaced Lieutenant Colonel James D. Alger, and Lieutenant Colonel John K. Waters was the executive officer as well as a code user (CU).[1] Winfrey assumed that Waters had sent the message.

Winfrey felt that, under the circumstances, a higher authority should be involved in this issue, and he telephoned Colonel J. Edward Johnston, commanding officer of MIS-X, for a meeting at Johnston's office. The following day, Winfrey arrived at the Pentagon to meet with Colonel Catesby ap Jones, who was now deputy chief of the Military Intelligence Service; Colonel Russell Sweet, chief of Captured Personnel and Matériel (formerly the Prisoner of War Branch); and Johnston.

In addressing the meeting, Colonel Jones produced a recent memo from MI-9 reporting that Heinrich Himmler had petitioned Hitler to let the SS control the POW camps. Himmler argued that the Luftwaffe guarding the air force camps and the Wehrmacht guarding the ground-officer Oflagen were too soft on POWs. He maintained that a tougher policy toward POWs, even going so far to cite any untoward POW behavior as a crime against the Reich, would result in fewer escapes and better camp control.

Colonel Sweet then advised the officers that the camp commandant at Oflag 64 was a Colonel Schneider, whom MIS-X believed served only as a figurehead. Schneider was an officer in the German Army Reserve, and intelligence information indicated that he frequently allowed his subordinate officers to countermand his orders. It was suspected that the real power lay with Captain Gunther Zimmerman, the camp security officer, a strong

Nazi party man and an enthusiastic supporter of Himmler's policies.[2]

Sweet reported an incident involving Zimmerman in which four American officers were being marched under guard to the hospital in town for treatment. They were ordered by their guards not to walk on the sidewalk, but to use the street amid the horse droppings. The officers felt that this was humiliating and in violation of the Geneva Convention, which required that POWs be treated humanely. The guards relented, allowing the officers to use the sidewalks. Zimmerman, upon hearing of this matter, brought charges against the four POWs as criminals of the Reich and requested the death sentence. The officers were brought to trial and acquitted, but Zimmerman had made his point.[3]

Upon hearing this account and others from Sweet, Colonel Jones decided that a further study of POW camp activities was necessary and indicated that he would make a meticulous search of his files for other such stories. He directed Johnston and Sweet to investigate their department files carefully as well as to determine how widespread this new German policy had become and to what degree it might be endangering the lives of POWs. He then recommended that they all meet back in his office in a week.

By May 20, six more signals had arrived from Oflag 64, all from different CUs. As Bedini decoded them, the impact of what he was reading began to overwhelm him:

1. DETAILED STUDY SHOWS FEASIBILITY RESCUE ENTIRE CAMP BY PLANE PD

2. TOTAL PRISONERS NOT OVER 400 PD AVAILABLE GERMAN FORCES IN AREA WEAK PD

3. AIR CORPS OFFICERS SAY FIELD NORTH EDGE CAMP SUITABLE LANDING FORTS PD

4. GUARD STRENGTH 155 PD ARMED RIFLE PD

AUTOMATIC RIFLE FOUR CORNERS OF CAMP
TOWER PD

5. INSIDE CONTACT CAN CUT TOWN COMMUNI-
CATIONS PD

6. 386 OFFICERS MOSTLY GROUND FORCES PD[4]

Once again, Winfrey carried these signals to the Pentagon for another special meeting. On the strength of these messages, Brigadier General H. A. Kroner, chief of MIS, was also present. After half an hour of open discussion by the group, the general proved himself to be a man of action who wasted neither time nor words, declaring, "The man on the spot is in the best position to make a decision. Colonel Drake and Colonel Waters are reliable senior officers, clearly trained and battle tested. Send them the damn guns. As for the rescue . . . we'll buck that upstairs for the Chief of Staff to decide. But signal 64 to take no action until they hear further, unless loss of life is imminent."

The next morning the six signals were reproduced to thirty-two different departments within the British and American armed services that might be involved in a rescue effort if it became a reality.[5] Priority photographic flights were ordered over Schubin from London to determine accurately if the fields north of Oflag 64 were capable of handling B-17s. Air force personnel were quizzed as to how fast B-17s could get on the ground in an open field, and thirty hand-picked paratroopers in London began a crash program to perfect low-level jumps and seize a guardhouse that might be occupied with as many as 130 sleeping guards. The files of known resistance workers in the Schubin area were combed for possible local collaborators in the plan. General Kroner then instructed Colonel Jones to have a workable rescue plan ready within a week.

At the same time, Winfrey, having returned to 1142, summoned Shoemaker to his office and ordered him to change into civilian clothes and prepare for a trip to Baltimore. It had been determined that .22-caliber Colt Woodsman automatic pistols would be the best weapons to send to Oflag 64. Shoemaker was to visit sporting goods stores to locate and buy two such guns, each to have an extra ammunition clip and a box of long rifle cartridges. He was given $200 in cash from the office safe and reminded to secure a receipt for the purchases.

Getting the guns that Shoemaker purchased into the prison camp would require ingenuity. The parcels sent under the names of fictitious humane societies would not do, as there was no way to secrete guns in such parcels— and even if there were, detection by the Germans would forever end the use of such an effective way of sending basic escape and evasion materials into the camps. Winfrey decided to use a bold tactic that had recently proven successful in limited shipments to POWs. If the request from Oflag 64 were approved by the Pentagon, Winfrey would ship the guns in packages that the British referred to as "Dynamites" and MIS-X called "Super-Dupers." These parcels had been used sparingly, on a trial basis, by the British, as they required cooperation from the POWs themselves for safe delivery.

Such parcels were the result of requests from the camps for contraband that could not be concealed in the regular parcels, owing to weight or size or both. POWs were asking for civilian clothes, especially those with a European cut; large maps of Europe; wire cutters; radios; and large sums of money. In one instance, a camp even asked for a hand-operated printing press, complete with type, inks, and paper.

Each Super-Duper was crammed with escape devices, with no effort made to conceal the contents. If opened, contraband would be plainly visible. The packages were always addressed to nonexistent POWs, from a return address in variously located U.S. cities. Using different locations required that the packages each have a postal cancellation stamp matching the city of origin. MIS-X arranged for this to be done through the services of the two postal supervisors who were currently handling its packages out of the Baltimore post office.

Safe delivery of the Super-Dupers depended on alerting the POWs through letter code and BBC broadcasts to expect their arrival. The forewarned POWs would then be expected to take possession of the parcel before it was examined at the camp by a German inspector. To assist the POWs in this effort, Super-Dupers were packed in used but substantial cardboard boxes and wrapping paper, secured with knotted pieces of twine, to give them a homemade look, suggesting that they were "comforts" from a next-of-kin.

During the war next-of-kins would receive a notice from the War Department that their relative was a POW. After presenting this notice at the local post office, they would receive a tag each month authorizing them to send one eleven-pound parcel, postage free, to the internee. MIS-X obtained a copy of one of these tags, and Hitchcock counterfeited it so that Super-Dupers could be shipped under the cover of next-of-kin packages. MIS-X consequently also referred to these parcels as next-of-kin packages, or NKs.

The day after Shoemaker returned with the guns, the first item of business at the Warehouse was to obtain two used cardboard boxes from the rear of the building to begin building NK parcels for the pistols. Corporal Peterson lined each box with a bed sheet and then placed one pistol in each, wrapped in heavy wax paper. He then placed two pairs of socks into each box, on top of the pistols. A spare clip and carton of shells were sandwiched between a pair of men's cotton gloves and placed over the socks. Finally, the remaining section of the liner sheets was folded over the items to ensure a snug fit and prevent movement or rattling of the contents. The boxes were sealed with heavy tape and wrapped in the used wrapping paper and twine.

Two counterfeit NK postage-free address tags were taken from stock; Peterson hand-addressed one to Lieutenant Leonard Grimm, and Shoemaker wrote the other to Captain Thomas Howard. Both of these names were fictitious, used after a check of the Red Cross list of POWs at Oflag 64 confirmed that no one held in the camp had similar names.

Winfrey then gave Shoemaker a memo for delivery to Bedini in the Creamery across the street. It instructed Bedini to prepare a secret signal and cable it to MI-9, who was then to transmit it over the BBC to alert the POWs at Oflag 64 that they should take the parcels addressed to Grimm and Howard before they passed by the camp censor. The message was to indicate that arrival of the packages should be expected within fourteen days.

To protect this shipment further, Winfrey relied on the special relationship MIS-X had with the army air corps, which flew material into Lisbon weekly for the U.S. embassy. Lisbon, the capital of a neutral country, was a hotbed of spy activity, and the United States had a larger-than-usual military attaché department stationed there. On occasion, the corps allowed an MIS-X parcel or two to be carried aboard their regular courier flights to Lisbon. Winfrey prearranged for these high-priority parcels to be placed on one of the planes. Upon arrival in Lisbon, the plane would be met by an intelligence agent who would take possession of the parcels and pass them on to a contact, who would get them into the Portuguese postal system. The parcels would then pass through Spain and France and, within a week, be worked into the German postal system, where they would then be delivered to Oflag 64 in Schubin.

Within two weeks, the parcels arrived as scheduled at the Schubin railroad depot with other camp mail, and the freight car carrying the packages was shunted to a siding to await off-loading. The Geneva Convention specified that officers were not required to work as POWs, but at most camps a few volunteered to work on mail duty to be in a position to remove "hot" parcels secretly. To their German captors, the officers appeared to be doing this work grudgingly but benevolently; they suggested that the presence of Americans during mail delivery would eliminate any accusations of German pilferage.

When the Germans were advised that a freight car of parcels was awaiting unloading, consequently, Captain James H. Dicks and Lieutenants Royal Lee and Amon Carter were driven, under guard, over the two miles of cobblestone road to the depot in an old German army truck.

As the men proceeded with the unloading, the two German guards and driver relaxed, as they were now outside of the camp and could enjoy a cigarette and idle conversation. Alerted to the NK shipment by the BBC broadcast, the three American officers, virtually ignored by the guards, began to go about their task in their routine manner. While Captain Dicks stood to one side of the freight car door with a clipboard, one of the other officers climbed into the railcar and began handing parcels to the other officer, who stacked the packages in the waiting truck. As each package was passed from the railcar, the name of the addressee was called out, and Dicks listed it on his clipboard. When the names Grimm and Howard were called out, however, Dicks only pretended to add the names to his list. In fact they were omitted, and the two packages were placed on the truck so as to be easily retrieved at the next stage of the delivery process.

After the loaded truck arrived at Oflag 64, it passed through the first of three barbed-wire fences that surrounded the camp and stopped at the *Vorlager* (receiving area), where several POWs were waiting to assist in the unloading. The truck was then emptied, with Dicks using verbal and visual cues to indicate to the new men the special parcels, which were once again placed so as to be accessible for easy recovery.

The censoring process then began, with two POWs standing at one end of a long table in the *Vorlager* and the German censor sitting at the opposite end. As one POW set a package on the table, the other cut the bindings and tape and pushed it toward the censor. Soon the packages were being opened faster than the censor could examine them, and a row of boxes extended the entire length of the table.

As each parcel was approved by the censor and confirmed by Dicks, a POW then moved it next to the *Vorlager* exit door. When this pile had grown sufficiently, Dicks suggested that everyone take a smoke and coffee break. The censor was quite agreeable, knowing that he would be included and be treated by the POWs to an American cigarette, a cup of real coffee, and if lucky, an American candy bar.

Upon Dicks's suggestion for a break, the POWs began to gather nonchalantly around a table and chairs off to one side of the room. As one began busily lighting a Sterno heater, another went to get water for the coffee. Meanwhile, a third POW began engaging the censor in small talk at the table, offering him a smoke at the same time. As the censor accepted the cigarette, the man lighting the stove handed him the lit match he was using. The two POWs, therefore, were now almost directly in front of the censor: one handing him a cigarette, the other handing him a match.

As this was going on, the two POWs working at the receiving table were also busy performing their roles in the scenario. When the suggestion for a break was made, each selected one of the contraband boxes, placed it on the table in the customary fashion, and cut the bindings and tape. The men began casually walking along the table, as if to join their comrades at the break area. Unnoticed, however, they were pushing the two parcels along with them as they walked. As the German censor leaned over to accept the lit match, the two "hot" parcels were snatched off the table and placed on the neighboring pile of already approved parcels. Then, appearing to straighten the pile, the POWs buried the now secure parcels by stacking other boxes on top of them. They then joined the others for coffee and a cigarette.

When the day's receiving was completed, the officers loaded the two special boxes onto a two-wheeled handcart along with about fifty other packages and pushed the cart through the main gate and into the compound for delivery.

The first stage of the mass escape plan had gone without a hitch: the guns had arrived safely.

The second stage was also moving on schedule. On May 27 Major General Clayton Bissell, assistant chief of staff G-2, chaired a meeting at the Pentagon consisting of the heads of MIS, MIS-X, and the Captured Personnel and Matériel Department, along with their subordinate staff officers. General Bissell advised the group that he represented George C. Marshall, chief of staff, and that following a review of the rescue plan that the group proposed, he would report the findings to General Marshall.

Colonel Jones was the first to read his report. He indicated that Lieutenant General Carl Spaatz, commanding the army air corps in London, had agreed to supply the required twenty B-17s and crew for the rescue mission. The 101st Airborne had thirty hand-picked men, armed with automatic weapons, ready for the predawn low-level jump on the guardhouse. In addition, the medical department would provide four medical corpsmen for the mission. Polish resistance had been contacted by radio and had promised to provide twenty-five men to mark the jump zone with flashlights and then join in the assault and cut the camp telephone lines. Meteorologists were giving the Schubin area special attention and reporting twice daily to the air corps. Jones then concluded by saying that the POWs would receive their instructions in a coded message over the BBC. The camp had a radio, sent months earlier by MIS-X, and nightly broadcasts from England were monitored by a member of the camp's escape committee. The POWs were to begin executing their plan one hour before dawn on the day following a BBC broadcast in which the phrase "Give me liberty or give me death" was used.

After an hour of further discussion of this plan, General Bissell felt that all precautions and contingencies had been properly planned and adjourned the meeting to make his report to General Marshall. Two days later, however, Jones received word that Secretary of War Stimson had offered his congratulations to the POWs for their daring and initiative but had rejected the plan because it was too risky. An unexpected German column had appeared in the area, and Stimson feared that, if the rescue attempt failed, the German troops would annihilate the rescuers and the POWs in the camp. He was also concerned that the twenty B-17s sitting on the ground near the camp, ready to transport the POWs, would be helpless against any sudden air or ground attack, and as the approaching German column indicated, German troop movement was too unpredictable to take chances.[6]

Stimson's decision engendered mixed emotions in everyone who had been involved in the escape plan. At 1142 the men were especially disappointed—they had labored hard and confidentially to perfect their part in the escapade and had favored carrying it through.

Forty-three years later the author interviewed General John K. Waters in his home at Potomac, Maryland. We sat in the den before a crackling fire, and the general recounted his POW days. The passing of the years had not dimmed his memory of the hardships of imprisonment, nor of the comrades who had shared those hardships with him. "Good men," he said. "Damn good men."

Military memorabilia filled the room: photos of men in uniform; small brass bugles from bygone cavalry days; defused artillery shells; a glass case with an incredible collection of medals, neatly displayed. Next to the fireplace stood an orange army flag with the four gold stars of a full general. Regrettably, the two pistols were not there.

Escape aids carriers. The brush handle held compass and maps. The *G* on the magnetized razor blade pointed north when balanced on a string. *(RAF Museum, Hendon, England, and U.S. Playing Card Company, Cincinnati)*

Shoe heel carried a map and ID photo. *(RAF Museum, Hendon, England, and U.S. Playing Card Company, Cincinnati)*

Escape map segments were hidden in a deck of cards; when pieced together, they make a full map. Chess piece carried money or compass. *(RAF Museum, Hendon, England, and U.S. Playing Card Company, Cincinnati)*

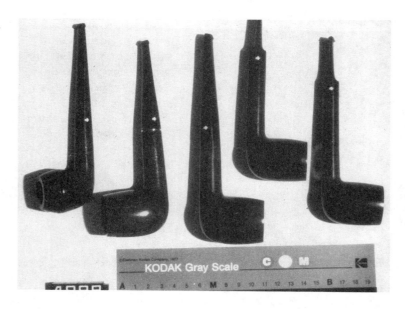

Kaywoodie pipes carried pencil-clip compasses as an X
ray of the pipes reveals the position. *(Silvio A. Bedini)*

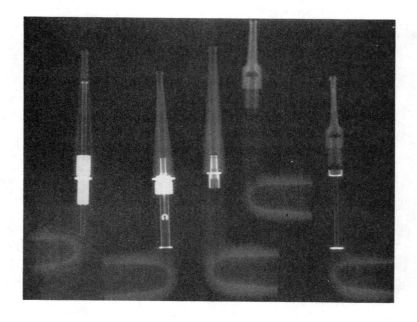

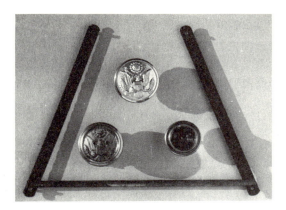

A gigili medical saw will cut through steel bars. The hollow button was unscrewed to retrieve compass; ten million were distributed. *(USAFA Library)*

MIS-X had manufacturers hide radio components inside baseballs and softballs. X ray of baseball shows the outline of the metal capsule that housed radio components. *(Author's collection)*

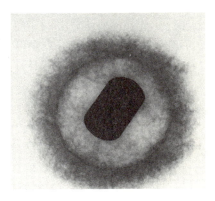

14

———✕———✕———

PARCELS FOR "RINGLING, BARNUM, AND BAILEY"

A THUNDERBOLT HIT MIS-X on June 2, 1944, when Brigadier Norman Crockatt sent Winfrey a copy of a letter that MI-9 had received from the International Red Cross in Geneva. The IRC said that they had received a complaint from German authorities regarding contraband found in parcels addressed to British POWs. The parcels had been sent to the camps from three different humanitarian organizations in England: Lewis's Ltd., the British Local Ladies Comfort Society, and the Lancashire Penny Fund.[1] These were but three of the thirty-six fictitious societies that the British, with their huge budget and large staff, were using to flood POW camps with E&E materials. With such an enormous operation, it stood to reason that sooner or later the law of averages would catch up with them and something would be discovered.

In a cover letter to Winfrey, however, Crockatt indicated that he was going to feign ignorance of the violations in hopes that the matter would blow over and be seen as simply an overeagerness on the part of little old ladies in well-meaning societies. "We have sent a cable

to the IRC in acknowledgment of their note," he wrote
to Winfrey. "But we can do nothing until they send us a
sample of the packing for our evaluation."[2] But before
the IRC could pursue the situation further, it was advised by the Germans that the three British societies
were hereafter restricted from sending any more parcels
into Germany, and the matter was dropped.

Winfrey, however, was uneasy about how casually
the British were handling this situation, as MIS-X was
about to start sending more of the vulnerable NK parcels. He had received numerous requests from POWs for
cameras to be sent into the camps, along with film, developing chemicals, and photographic paper. POWs
could use the cameras for a multitude of purposes, but
the most immediate was to take mug shots for fake IDs.
Cameras, however, could not be loaded in humanitarian
packages.

Winfrey wanted to obtain the most versatile camera
available and called the Kodak Company in Rochester,
New York, for assistance. Without identifying himself or
his purpose, Winfrey spoke with a technician at the company and learned that the Kodak 35 was their most full-
service camera that was also simple to operate. Kodak,
the official said, was engaged in war production and had
no backup stock to sell. "However," the representative
said, "that model is very popular, and you should not
have too much trouble locating one in a good camera
store."

Shoemaker, summoned into Winfrey's office by Corporal Paul Huss, arrived to find a large pile of $20 bills
on the desk. Pushing a prepared receipt toward Shoemaker, Winfrey told him, "Sign for the money. There's
$300. In your travels, have you noticed any cameras in
the stores?"

"No sir, not offhand," Shoemaker responded, "but I
haven't been looking for them either."

"Kodak 35 is the brand and model we need,"

Winfrey continued. "I want you to find a dozen along with all the film developer and paper you can lay your hands on. And be sure you get a receipt!"

On the third day of his search, Shoemaker entered a large department store after dropping off twenty bags of parcels at the Baltimore post office. As he approached the camera department, Shoemaker's hopes rose: the shelves were well stocked with cameras, tripods, lights, and other accessories.

The salesman introduced himself as Mr. Crawford and indicated that, indeed, he had the Kodak 35, "right here on the shelf." He handed it to Shoemaker for inspection, but Shoemaker told him, "No, it isn't necessary for me to examine it. That's the one I want . . . but do you have any more?"

"Well, yes, I think I have another," responded the clerk, somewhat taken by surprise. "But I assure you, sir, there's nothing wrong with the camera you're holding."

"Oh, I'm sure it's okay," Shoemaker said, smiling enthusiastically, pleased with the discovery of this windfall, "I would just like to have three or four more if you have them."

"My, my," Crawford stammered. And then, looking somewhat suspiciously at Shoemaker, he added, "If you will excuse me for a moment, I will check the back room," and disappeared through a door. Several moments later, he reappeared, stating, "I do have three more, sir, but it will take a minute for the boy to get them off the high shelf."

The minutes seemed to drag as Crawford puttered at the far end of the counter, leaving Shoemaker to entertain himself examining the items in the showcase. Then, as Shoemaker was squatting down looking at the equipment in the bottom of the case, he heard a voice behind him say, "Mr. Crawford, I have called the FBI, and they are sending a man right over. Where is the spy?"

Shoemaker needed no one to tell him that he was the object of this person's inquiry, and rising quickly to his feet and not looking backward, he walked rapidly from the store.

That afternoon, Shoemaker returned to 1142 and, as Winfrey was away at the Pentagon, he told his tale of woe to Major Leo Crosson, who laughingly said, "Well, hell, boy, that ain't nothing to get excited about. After all, the most they can do to you in a time of war is shoot you—and you ain't nothin' but a damn Yankee anyway."

By the end of the week, however, six cameras had been purchased along with accessories, and Winfrey immediately ordered Bedini to send off a coded letter to Colonel Charles Goodrich at South Compound in Stalag Luft III, which was to read: "Detour three parcels for Ringling Barnum and Bailey PD Urgent PD."

Then, because it was imperative that the letter reach the camp before the parcels, Winfrey instructed Bedini to dispatch the message by air mail to Sweden, knowing that it should then arrive at the camp in about three weeks. The parcels, which would travel over the ocean via convoy, would take four to six weeks to arrive at the camp.

Excitement began to grow at 1142, as once again an NK was being shipped out and MIS-X had no idea if the POWs at Stalag Luft III would be able to safely keep these parcels away from the German censors. Winfrey did know, however, that the POWs at Stalag Luft III had the greatest opportunity to pull off this risky venture as they, having been exposed to the British POW camp operation when British and American POWs were held together in the North Compound, had already established a sophisticated camp E&E committee.

Upon their arrival at the camp, the NKs, with their highly visible contraband items, had to be somehow moved past the German censors. Once inside the camp, the packages then had to be hidden from camp inspec-

134 — THE ESCAPE FACTORY

tions and even the general awareness of other POWs. Like the NK parcels containing pistols that had been sent to Oflag 64, the packages would have to be intercepted and so would have to be packaged carefully. Winfrey and Crosson therefore supervised every facet of their packing for Stalag Luft III.

Three old cardboard boxes, used wrapping paper, and twine were gathered by Hitchcock, and Peterson brought in three single-sized bed sheets. Each box was lined with a sheet, leaving extra material to cover the top of the contents. Two cameras were then placed in each box, cushioned on the bottom and sides by the sheet. A pair of rolled-up civilian socks filled the spaces around the cameras, and two more pairs of socks were laid flat over the tops.

Peterson then brought the parcels to the scales, where they weighed out at eight and one-half pounds. Because the maximum parcel weight was eleven pounds, another two and a half pounds of materials were needed to fill the packages. Hitchcock suggested that a carton of cigarettes and some candy bars be added. They then weighed ten and a half pounds, which Winfrey decided was enough.

The third box was now filled with camera and developing accessories. Twelve boxes of film were packed in a double row over the sheet so as to fit snugly. Four cans of chemicals were then placed in the box, their screw tops taped to guard against loosening and leakage. As with the cameras, rolled-up socks were placed around the cans to keep them from rattling. Four packs of photo paper were then put on top of the chemicals. Crosson requested a weighing of the package, which came to ten pounds. Two enlarger lenses and six candy bars were added to the box, which now weighed ten and a half pounds.

Winfrey nodded his approval, and Peterson folded the sheet ends over the contents and closed the box, as

Hitchcock supplied the tape to seal the flaps. When the three parcels had been taped, wrapped, and tied, they were ready for the address tags. Since Peterson's handwriting was atrocious, Winfrey had Crosson address the first tag saying, "It goes to Lieutenant Harvey Barnum at South Compound, Stalag Luft III, Sagan, Germany. Of course, no such officer exists by that name in the camp, so if the parcel is discovered by the Germans, they can't retaliate. And if the Huns trace it to the sender, they will be rewarded by finding a vacant lot."

Hitchcock, whose home was in Cleveland, Ohio, readily volunteered an address he knew to be a vacant lot, and Crosson wrote it on the tag as the return address. Corporal Huss and Sergeant Harris from the shop provided blind addresses from their home towns for the other two parcels. As Winfrey and Crosson watched, Peterson brought his tray of censor's stamps from the safe. Selecting three different numbers, he stamped each parcel. When bagged and delivered to the Baltimore post office, one of the two supervisors would apply the postal cancellation mark that would match the return address.

It would be weeks before the men at MIS-X could expect any news of whether these particularly dangerous packages reached their intended recipients undetected.

15

---×---×---

COMMITTEE WORK

By the end of June 1944, the Allied invasion of Europe was three weeks old. The ground forces were tenaciously fighting for their toehold on Normandy's shores while the air arm roared overhead, pulverizing Germany's road and rail systems. The Germans reported taking twenty-five thousand prisoners and boasted that they would throw the Allied armies back into the sea. General Dwight Eisenhower responded, "We have a million men ashore, and by God we are going to stay there."

With the British and Americans on the west, the Russians on the east, and POWs in the middle, Hitler, despite his bravado, had a full plate. Determined to eliminate at least one of these threats, he issued his Kommando Order, aimed at all Allied POWs. "Escape is no longer a sport," he said, and proclaimed the infamous Death Zones throughout Europe in areas where munitions, armaments, and experimental plants were located. A POW caught in a Death Zone would be immediately executed.

The Allied objective of making the POW an active

resister was having its desired effect but not without consequences. The nets were tightening around the Third Reich, and the Third Reich was beginning to tighten its nets around the POWs. POW camp activities were curtailed, and food rations were again cut to less than eighteen hundred calories per day per man. Arrests and trials of POWs for minor offenses increased and in each case the German prosecutor asked for the death sentence "for the destruction of Reich property."

In light of these new penalties, the United States and Britain issued a coded-letter order to all POWs: "Escape is no longer a duty, but an individual prerogative."[1]

Colonel Charles Goodrich, SAO of the newly occupied South Compound at Stalag Luft III, received the decode from one of his CUs and ordered it read to all personnel. They responded by unanimously voting to continue their resistance on the barbed-wire front. Upon hearing this, Lieutenant Colonel Albert P. Clark, Jr., now the "Big X" at the American compound, met with his escape committee and ordered an increase in activities. POWs in the tailoring factory were put to work shaving army blankets they had received, unbeknownst to them, from MIS-X. Running a razor across the blankets, they were able to produce a material not unlike serge in men's suits, from which the tailors then made civilian suits and coats. Men with dexterous fingers and keen eyesight went to work in the forgery factory. One such POW, Lieutenant James Billig, worked eight hours a day for a month using indelible pencils and colored inks, forging a set of ID papers that passed Gestapo inspections four times before the escaper using them was finally caught and returned to the compound. Billig recently recalled his work on the camp's forgery committee:

> I was quite proud of my part of that job. But most of it was done by a man named Katz. I

don't remember his first name, but he came from California. It was tedious work—taking us a month just to get up a good set of escape documents.

Clark was very tight on security. If you were not directly involved in some covert activity, you never knew it was going on. You had to be directly involved to get it.

I was not a code user until after I got to camp. Clark picked me, and another CU was assigned to teach me a new American code that had come in some way. Then Clark put all the CUs in one cubicle for security—we all had to help each other because the codes were difficult to write. You had to use certain words that would properly fit the general tone of the letter as well as the secret message. We needed to help each other to find the right words.

We were given a cubicle on the side of the barracks that had the best sunlight, so we could see to do the fine work. It was meticulous work. While one CU rested his eyes, he would stand security lookout while another CU worked on the code. We always had lots of security guards out in case a ferret or guard showed up. We called them "goons."

Clark had a regular duty roster whereby other POWs took turns standing two-hour security shifts at the doors on each end of the barracks. If a "goon" showed up, the security guy would detain him with a question or some distraction. The CU on security at the cubicle door would see this and alert us, giving us a minute to button up.

We had a few pens to use on the forgeries that some of the men had been able to keep. Ink, however, was the biggest problem. The men working the hospital would steal Mercurochrome, or we would pulverize indelible pencils in a mixture of alcohol or glycerin. Clark would bribe some guards to carry in colored inks and pen points. For the fine work, we had a flashlight lens for a magnifying glass.

The stamps we needed were carved from a rubber heel sent in the clothing parcels. We had a guy with gifted fingers who could carve the stamps with a razor blade. We never had much trouble keeping updated on stamps, as the "goons" all had to have their papers stamped regularly, and Major [Jerry] Sage was somehow able to get us copies of their papers.

About the time our operation got going really good, though, the parcels we were receiving started including printed documents and the materials we needed. All we had to do then was to enter someone's name, a date, and forge a signature.[2]

Billig never knew that the parcels he received were sent by MIS-X. He never knew, in fact, where they came from.

CAPTAIN JOHN M. BENNETT went to work in the compass factory, having learned the painstaking procedure of his trade under an Australian named Al Hake when they had been held together in North Compound. Recalling his work, Bennett said:

It was quite unique. To begin with, we used broken Bakelite phonograph records. It was a material which with heat became very soft and molded with ease. Our mold was a bed board with a hole in it about one and one-quarter inch in diameter. We would put the soft Bakelite over the hole and then push a section of it through the hole. It was easy, doing this, to form the warm Bakelite into a cup about one-half inch deep. Then, with the plug still in the form, we pressed the Bakelite onto a metal disk that imprinted the words "Made in Stalag Luft III" onto the bottom of the cup that held each compass we made.

I would next glue a bunch of old razor blades into a double line on a board in such a way that the two legs of a child's horseshoe magnet could be drawn across each line of blades simultaneously. I then stroked the blades in the same direction for three to four hours. At the end of that time, I'd induced permanent magnetism into the blades.

I then used a window hinge as a precision vice and broke the blades into precisely sized magnets.

Compass cards were then made from cardboard, into which I drilled a hole exactly in the center. Warm Bakelite was pushed through the hole so as to extend out of the top of the card. A sharp lead pencil created a tiny cavity in the point, so the compass card could be suspended on a phonograph needle. Using broken window glass, I cut a top for each compass under water with a pair of scissors. A short strip of cardboard served as a spacer for the glass to sit on.

It worked beautifully.[3]

Everyone who could work on an escape committee did something. Often a POW worked on several committees. Captain Bennett, for example, not only made compasses but was in charge of the disposition of security materials that entered the camp. "I created the 'hidey-holes,'" he recalled years later, "where contraband could lie undetected by the German searches. You know, the Germans must have had X committees in mind when they built those barracks, as each one had double walls separating the rooms. We would just move one wall out a bit into the room so as to create a cavity between the two walls. Once a trap door was cut and camouflaged in the wall, the space behind it made an excellent place to hide contraband because the Germans would never tear down a wall and search behind it. They were very careful never to damage their own property."[4]

But working with materials supplied to the camp from outside was not sufficient. POWs also needed to obtain materials from within and around the camps, and Stalag Luft III was no exception. Clark therefore set up a procurement committee and appointed Lieutenant Alvin W. "Sammy" Vogtle to head it. He and his helpers were to acquire necessary equipment to round out the supplies for any approved escape plans. They would do this through outright theft or by using "tame" guards who could be bribed into carrying contraband into the camps.

On one occasion, Lieutenant Vogtle stood watching a group of German civilian workmen building a concrete slab. Fellow committee member Major David Jones passed by and paused to comment on how handy a sack of cement would be in preparing a tunnel entry. Fifteen minutes later, as Jones was sitting in his cubicle, Vogtle entered, carrying a heavy object concealed beneath a blanket. Without a grunt, Vogtle placed the bundle on the floor, removed the blanket, and walked away without saying a word—leaving a bag of cement in front of Jones.[5]

Owing to exploits such as this, Sammy Vogtle and his crew soon became known as "Sammy and His Forty Thieves." Sometimes, however, they overachieved. Vogtle once stole the entire tool kit from the German camp electrician. Unfortunately, and unbeknownst to Vogtle, the electrician was also one of the best sources of military information that the escape committee's intelligence unit had. The tools were quickly returned to the informant.[6]

His camp colleagues believed there was nothing that Vogtle could not obtain, and his activities in the camp elicited not only amazement and admiration, but gratitude for the lives he was saving.

When once asked by escape committee member Major Jerry Sage if he could obtain one of the new gate passes that the Germans were using, Vogtle asked Sage for a quart of the major's "home brew," and then told his bunk mates to clear the cubicle for a couple of hours. Then he sat patiently waiting for his "tame" ferret to make his usual visit. When the guard showed up, Vogtle offered him schnapps instead of the usual cup of coffee. The guard eagerly accepted. Four hours and several cups of black coffee later, the ferret was sober enough to walk out the front gate in time to end his shift . . . and his pay book, ID card, and new gate pass were safely back in his pocket.

On another occasion, a German general visited the POW camp and insisted on being driven directly into the center of the camp, refusing to walk from the gate. The camp commandant, Colonel Friedrich-Wilhelm von Lindeiner, tried to persuade the general to walk and leave his vehicle outside the compound, as the POWs were known to be adroit thieves. But the general scoffed at the suggestion, saying that there would be no trouble— his driver was an alert and excellent German soldier.

Once in the center of the compound, the general cautioned his driver to be most vigilant and then departed with the commandant for an inspection of the camp. As soon as the general left his car, a Mercedes-Benz, it was surrounded by POWs, who admired and exclaimed over it and struck up conversations with the driver as he sat stiffly in his seat, clutching the steering wheel. Eventually the driver was coaxed into raising the hood to show off the engine. As the POWs milled around, the driver

rushed to fill the pan with fresh water. Williams, realizing that his job was to distract these two Germans, quickly took a chair next to the sergeant and brought out his pack of cigarettes.

Bell, meanwhile, by prearrangement with Rosner, walked to the head of the receiving table where he shielded Rosner, who quickly removed one of the hot parcels that he had seen Bell put on the table. Rosner placed it in the approved pile; with the box flaps open, Rosner could clearly see the big camera lying inside the box, and his heart skipped a beat. Joining Bell, Rosner casually walked with him over to the break table.

Williams, engaged with the sergeant, had not seen anything, but glimpsing the expressions on his three assistants' faces, he knew they had accomplished something. With a feeling of relief, he reached for his musette bag and brought out a small jar of instant coffee and set it on the table.

The men finished their coffee and cigarettes and soon returned to their jobs. With half an hour to go before lunch, the stack of packages was dwindling and Bell once again nodded to Captain Williams. Williams suggested a cigarette break and followed the sergeant to the break table. The guard was standing by the exit, watching the POWs in the compound. As he turned to join the censor and Williams for a cigarette, he caught Bell by surprise, as Bell was almost upon him with an open hot parcel under one arm. Without missing a beat, Bell smiled and extended four candy bars to the guard with his free hand. Caught off balance himself now, the guard grabbed the prized chocolate bars, turning his back to the room as he covertly stuffed the booty into his shirt pocket. When he turned back to the room, he saw Bell, Pollak, and Rosner standing in front of him and felt sure that something unusual had just occurred but was not sure what it was. Rosner, Pollak and Bell now joined the bemused guard, and the four walked over to the break table just as Williams was setting out four candy bars and two packs of cigarettes, which he divided between the two Germans.

Later, as Williams, Bell, Pollak, and Rosner were preparing to depart for lunch, the sergeant said to them, "Don't forget to take the parcels for your friends."

"Thank you for the reminder, Herr Feldwebel," Williams said, suppressing a smile. "I'm sure we would have forgotten them otherwise." He then picked up a parcel and smiled all the way back to his barracks.[8]

Two months later, Winfrey also smiled and breathed a welcomed sigh of relief as he read a coded letter from Stalag Luft III that read: "Received cameras PD Picture of German security officer developed beautifully PD."

SHORTLY AFTER THIS NK was received, Winfrey received a report that forced him to change the distribution of MIS-X's shipments. A first lieutenant by the name of William F. Higgins had been repatriated from Stalag Luft III, and he brought with him a report from Colonel Goodrich: "No more escape material to be sent to South Compound, please. So much is on hand now that storage space is acute."[9]

On May 19, 1943, Higgins had been a bombardier in a bomber group, departing from Chelveston, England, to bomb Kiel, Germany. The pilot of a B-17, Higgins was shot down by Me-110s six minutes after successfully bombing the assigned target. He remembered the copilot leaving the burning ship but had no recollection of his own evacuation. He was told that German civilians had picked him up after he had landed in a field. He was unconscious, suffering a concussion, and had a paralyzed left leg.

Higgins spent nearly a month in a hospital in Schleswig, Germany, receiving only perfunctory medical treatment. Other than what came in Red Cross parcels, the only food he had was barley soup. He recovered from the concussion, but his left leg remained paralyzed. Nevertheless, he was moved to Stalag Luft III, where the repatriation board was meeting. With Goodrich's assistance, Higgins was declared an invalid and repatriated out of Germany on the Swedish liner *Gripsholm*. Like other repatriates, he carried information from the POW CO to MIS-X:

The day before I left, Colonel Goodrich had me come to his room where he and Lieutenant Colonel Clark coached me on a long message I was to bring back. They impressed me not to talk to anyone, except an MIS-X officer. So, when Lieutenant Colonel Starr came aboard ship and told me he was MIS-X, I knew he was the officer I was to talk with and told the following story.

I was not aware that there was some means of communication with the War Department, nor realized the system was so extensive or efficient. Security is A-1, as not a hint was ever mentioned in the camp. Some men were trying to use their own private code to write home, but the German censors were catching most of them.

Messages giving the order "Stay put at collapse of Germany" have been received, and Colonel Goodrich says the camp will remain in place when the collapse occurs. But Colonel Goodrich wants the War Department to know that squadrons have been formed so as to meet any emergency. The POWs understand the SS is to shoot the POWs upon Germany's surrender, and Colonel Goodrich emphasized it is advisable to get the men out of camp and the area as soon as possible. There is also the possibility of reprisals by civilians, as they are angry at the bombing—plus very hungry.

Colonel Goodrich's only complaint is that

loaded parcels are arriving in camp ahead of the letter which warns of their arrival. This necessitates tracing the loaded items in the camp and taking them away from the men who received them. The men don't understand why this is done. The POW parcel officer, Captain Robert E. Williams, can spot most loaded parcels from the labels and manages to steal them. But it is hazardous.

In November of '43, three officers escaped from East Compound, and it is believed they reached England safely. But since the mass break in North Compound in March '44 where 50 POWs were shot by the Gestapo [the Great Escape], all attempts at escape and all tunneling in South Compound have ceased.[10]

Winfrey ordered an immediate cessation of loaded parcels to all camps until he could correct the problems indicated in Higgins's report. Continuing the flow of E&E materials to POWs was essential, but by failing to send coded letters to them in time to prepare for the shipments, he was putting the already endangered men at too much risk. Food parcels, however, would continue, as these were never loaded and provided a needed supplement to the POWs' often skimpy diet. Hereafter, only food and clothing parcels would be dispatched to South Compound of Stalag Luft III, as they had enough escape devices on hand. But coded letters continued to come in from other camps, carrying intelligence information and requesting E&E materials.

Winfrey now turned the focus of MIS-X's E&E activities toward these other camps.

16

—×——×——

MAKING THE MAIL

THREE POW CAMPS IN Europe had sent signals to 1142 requesting radios. It was contrary to Winfrey's policy to delay meeting such requests, but he had been withholding radios while Lieutenant James H. McTighe devised a new crystal set equipped with a radio dial knob. It could be concealed in a cribbage board and would easily pass censors when carried in society parcels. The sets would be superior to previous radios, as they permitted an operator to scan across the dial for different stations and select the one with the clearest reception. This option would be of great value to the POWs, as several Allied stations in North Africa that aired BBC broadcasts could actually be heard more clearly in eastern Europe than the original broadcasts from England could.

When a fourth signal came in from Stalag Luft VI requesting a radio, only four new radios had been completed, but Winfrey ordered them prepared for shipment. Stalag Luft VI, in East Prussia, was known to be a large camp, holding twenty-eight hundred American air gunners, and Winfrey did not want to make them wait until more new radios were produced. Moreover, Winfrey recognized the code user as Technical Sergeant Francis S. Paules, who was also the camp's POW leader, its Man of Confidence (MOC). He had been shot down on January 20, 1944, while on detached service to the Royal Canadian Air Force as a bombardier. Winfrey knew that, to implement his camp's escape activities, Paules needed a radio. Additionally, Paules had proven to be an invaluable source of intelligence information for MIS-X, and his intelligence was beyond question: he was the only POW who had ever been able to link up the censor's numbers that MIS-X was using with the coded letters and could recognize the latter the moment they entered the camp.[1]

Winfrey, already two weeks late in shipping the radios and anxious to get a radio to Paules, did not want to follow the normal shipping procedures. He telephoned the naval liaison officer at the Pentagon, who advised him that the next convoy to Europe would sail from Baltimore that night. The officer told Winfrey, "All cargo must be on board by 1800 hours." Winfrey then called the Baltimore post office, where the assistant postmaster informed him that the last mail from their station for the convoy would leave at 1500 hours.

Winfrey decided to ship the radio via the convoy and called in Shoemaker, advising him that a delivery had to be made to the Baltimore post office before 1500 hours. There would not be enough time to prepare a large shipment, but Winfrey knew that with Hitchcock and Shoemaker helping Peterson, the four radios plus five straight parcels to be sent along for cover could be ready by noon.

With a wartime speed of thirty-five miles per hour, the run to Baltimore would take two hours. U.S. Highway 1 was a narrow two-lane road that wound its way through several small hamlets dotted with traffic lights that had to be observed. The bald tires on the delivery truck always made Shoemaker anxious, and on this particular day, even though there would be reduced traffic because of gas rations and moderate speeds, Shoemaker found himself worrying about an accident.

As he entered the hamlet of Laurel, Maryland, the right rear tire blew out, and Shoemaker pulled to the exceptionally wide shoulder to make repairs. The clock continued ticking for the ten minutes it took him to mount the spare, and he was only too happy to pull back onto the highway to resume his trip. Almost immediately his left rear tire blew out, leaving him with no spare, twenty miles from Baltimore, with only an hour to get his three hot mailbags to the post office before 3:00 P.M.

Scanning his surroundings for a solution, Shoemaker noticed a blue sign up the road that had a white dog outline on it. He knew instantly that it was a Greyhound bus stop. Locking the truck, he pulled the three heavy mailbags two hundred yards up the highway and stood under the sign, waiting for the bus. "I must live right to receive such a blessing," he said to himself, as he saw a bus approaching after only a five-minute wait.

The driver was reluctant to allow Shoemaker to board with his three huge mailbags unless he paid the toll for his excess baggage. Shoemaker had never even considered the fare, and he suddenly realized that all he had was some small change in his pocket. Fearing a court martial if he missed the convoy, Shoemaker boldly picked up a bag of mail and threw it into the entry of the bus, quickly sending the other two bags after it. Then he scrambled aboard. Very determined, he looked the driver in the eye and said, "I am commandeering this bus in the name of the U.S. Postal Service. We are going to Baltimore, so take off, driver!"

The driver started to resist but was quickly quieted by Shoemaker's counter that the mailbags contained government high-priority documents, and the penalty for delaying the mail in time of war was a ten-year sentence at Leavenworth penitentiary. The driver, clearly intimidated by this, drove Shoemaker directly to the front door of the Baltimore post office. As Shoemaker dismounted with his mail, the driver demanded his name so that the incident could be reported to his company.

"Everybody in the post office knows me," Shoemaker said, looking over his shoulder. "It's James A. Farley."

Shoemaker then checked his watch and saw that it was ten minutes before three. Dragging the three bags to the loading area at the back of the building, Shoemaker called for a postal supervisor, telling him it was imperative that the bags be on the 3:00 P.M. truck.

"Don't worry," the supervisor said. "That truck is loading now, and I will see that these get on."

From the telephone book, Shoemaker then located the address of the First Service Command, which maintained a large garage in downtown Baltimore for the convenience of the many staff officers stationed in the city. Fortunately, it was close enough that he could walk to it. Shoemaker identified himself to the master sergeant on duty there as an intelligence agent working on a special assignment in civilian clothes with a civilian-looking vehicle, which had broken down. Shoemaker explained to the sergeant that his black truck was parked at Laurel with a flat tire and no spare. He then gave the sergeant the special phone number at the Pentagon and urged him to call Major Harris to confirm the story. Upon receiving confirmation of Shoemaker's identity, the sergeant sent out a repair truck to service Shoemaker's vehicle, while Shoemaker walked to the Ben Franklin store to pick up materials for MIS-X.

When Shoemaker returned to 1142 that evening, the gate guard must have alerted Winfrey by phone, as he was standing on the Warehouse loading dock when the little black truck came to a halt. "Well, Mr. Farley, I see you have returned," he said.

Shoemaker inferred that he might be in trouble for

impersonating the postmaster general of the United States. Nothing further, however, was ever said about the matter. But the episode brought to everyone's attention the similarities that existed between the operations of MIS-X and those of the POWs in the camps themselves. Both were working under delicate and secretive circumstances, where plans frequently changed by the minute and decisions were always accompanied by uncertainty.

17

INTERCEPTED

THE VIRGINIA WEATHER IN August 1944 was said to be
the warmest in years. The Potomac River, flowing only
three hundred yards from 1142, contributed to the high
humidity as the sun beat on the uninsulated Warehouse
roof. Because security prohibited opening windows or
doors, the technicians were bathed in sweat. Discussions
were terse, and some tempers matched the climbing mer-
cury.

In addition to the heat and humidity, the crew in the
Warehouse felt something else in the air, something sig-
nifying a change that was about to occur.

One noticeable difference was the presence on the
base of Major Leo Crosson. Ordinarily on the road obtaining money and purchasing supplies in remote areas,
he had now been at 1142 for a full week, looking in on
Corporal Peterson, conferring with Lieutenant McTighe
in the shop, visiting the Creamery, and checking Shoemaker's departures and arrivals in the truck.

The next curious occurrence was the promotion of
Winfrey to full colonel, Peterson to sergeant, and Shoe-

maker to corporal. These promotions were unusual for MIS-X; because of its top-level secrecy, it did not have a table of organization through which such matters were usually handled in the military. Winfrey explained that the ratings had been borrowed from Colonel Sweet's MIS-Y section.

More disconcerting news came in a letter forwarded to the Warehouse that the Pentagon had received from the International Red Cross in Switzerland. It stated that the Germans were protesting parcels intercepted by censors at Stalag Luft I at Barth, Germany, that contained contraband. The names of the addressees were not given, but the return addresses and the contents of the parcels were. The first, from H. A. Burns, 1219 Maple Street, Albany, New York, contained:

1 civilian trousers
1 complete radio w/parts
43 miniature compasses
1 wire cutter
1 combination pliers
12 steel saw blades
1 pocketknife
Several hundred German Reichmarks

A second parcel with a Richmond, Virginia, return address contained:

1 blue man's suit
1 white shirt
1 "B" battery for radio
1 flashlight battery
1 bottle of red ink
12 conterfeit forms
1,000 Reichmarks in paper money

The most blatant parcel of contraband was addressed to Lieutenant Carl C. Mackemer, with no camp number given. It contained:

1 Kodak camera
1 can of fixing slats
1 package of developer
3 rolls of film
1 package photographic paper
16 different counterfeit identification papers[1]

The German letter of protest was well founded, as the staff of 1142 knew that the discovered parcels were indeed MIS-X parcels—three of twelve NKs that had been dispatched two months prior. The crew in the Warehouse silently thanked the German government for unwittingly advising them that the remaining nine NKs had been successfully delivered.

The discovered NKs were a disappointment. But Winfrey knew that, with the hundreds of parcels that were being shipped, the law of averages dictated that sooner or later some of them would be detected. This was becoming increasingly possible given that the parcels sometimes arrived before the coded letter could alert the POWs to abscond with the packages. Mail service in Germany was growing more and more unpredictable, as the Allies were engaged in heavy bombing of rail and highway systems, often leaving German mail trains and trucks stranded for days.

The German government, meanwhile, was also using parcels to contact their POWs held in the United States. Instead of concealed escape aids, though, they sent propaganda messages boasting of how the Wehrmacht and Luftwaffe were driving the Allies back into the sea.[2] In a revealing reversal of the German POW policy, the U.S. government gave the German POWs access to radios so they could hear the real story for themselves.

Perhaps the most curious event at 1142 that August was the arrival of an army truck, which, by prearrangement, was met at the main gate by two MPs from the post's guard force. They escorted the truck to the loading dock at the Warehouse, where Winfrey and Peterson were waiting. After Winfrey signed for receipt of the delivery, Peterson was allowed to remove two heavy wooden crates from the truck and bring them into the Warehouse. Each of the crates weighed about 150 pounds and was bound with steel straps. Except for a long number stenciled on one side, the crates were unmarked. When Peterson inquired about the contents so as to identify the boxes for inventory, Winfrey simply told him, "Enter them as two wooden steel-bound crates," and told Peterson to place them in a far corner.

Two weeks passed uneventfully after the arrival of the mysterious boxes. During this time Major Crosson remained on duty at 1142, and the two crates remained, unopened, in the corner. Then, early one morning, the security door to the technical section of the Warehouse flew open, and Winfrey bounded in, calling for Peterson to move the boxes into the center of the room and for Hitchcock to fetch a crowbar and hammer.

The staff gathered around as Peterson broke the metal straps and pried off the wooden slats. As he folded back the heavy waxed-paper liner, stacks of orange-colored currency were revealed. "A million dollars," Winfrey explained casually to the startled crew. "A million dollars in Chinese yuan is in each box." Then, turning to Hitchcock with one of his rare smiles, he added, "Maurice, no reflection on your talents, but this is not toilet paper money. This is the real stuff."

When the lid was nailed back on and the metal bindings replaced, Winfrey ordered the boxes loaded into Shoemaker's truck. Then, pointing to Peterson and Hitchcock, he said, "You men be sure to wear your caps. And Shoemaker, stay in uniform. We are delivering these boxes."

Four hours later, the four men arrived at Bolling Field Air Force Base in Maryland. After checking Winfrey's ID, a gate guard directed the truck to a hangar, where four armed MPs took up positions at each corner of the truck as it came to a halt. Ten minutes later, an army truck arrived, escorted by two Jeeps carrying more MPs. A major dismounted from one of the Jeeps and exchanged IDs with Winfrey. Then, signing Winfrey's receipt, the major took possession of the two boxes and drove away.

As the convoy faded across the tarmac, Winfrey said, "They can have the headache of delivering it, but I will have the pleasure of spending it."

By the end of the week, Winfrey had made his comment clear. Calling the technical and correspondence sections together in the briefers' room, Winfrey bade everyone farewell. He was going to the South Pacific. Thousands of Red Cross and NK parcels had been shipped to Japan on the Swedish liner *Gripsholm,* but the Japanese were restricting mail delivery and most of the food parcels were being placed in storage sheds. Native vendors, however, were being allowed into POW camps to sell food, so Winfrey was going to try working directly with the vendors, paying them to deliver fresh fruits and vegetables inside the camps.

"I'm going to make a lot of natives rich," he said, "and Major Crosson is taking over at 1142 in my place." Then, with his customary terseness, he left the room.

The crew at MIS-X was astonished by this sudden disclosure. The war was in its third year, a crucial period. Hundreds of escape aids remained to be shipped; briefers needed to be updated and correspondence traffic maintained. A War Department memo had revealed that, by August 1944, 666 flying personnel who had been shot down since D day had returned safely to Allied control.[3] The Allied bombing of Germany, however, had been so severe that the briefers now had to instruct airmen to carry pistols. While doing so had been optional before, parachuting airmen were now considered enemies by German citizens and were apt to be met on the ground by irate civilians armed with pitchforks or clubs. If evasion was not feasible, airmen were instructed to surrender to a policeman or soldier.

The memo also indicated that the underground activity, particularly the escape railway—which MIS-X and MI-9 had set up in cooperation with the American OSS and the British SOE—was so active that an escaper or evader, once in their hands, had a better than fifty-fifty chance of arriving in England. With Allied penetration into France, the escape railway was bringing E&E men through the combat areas to freedom. The old escape route over the Pyrenees into Spain was now passing into history—except, ironically, that the Germans themselves were using it, as pockets of German ground forces in southern France, cut off by the invasion, were scaling the mountains to reach safety.[4]

Working with the Resistance movement in friendly countries, MIS-X and MI-9 units were coordinating much of the movement along the underground escape routes and were evacuating hundreds of escapers and evaders, often using torpedo boats and submarines.

Major Crosson was thus inheriting enormous responsibility when he was assigned to take over command of the MIS-X post at 1142. But his deep southern drawl, his perpetual smile, and his total lack of military formality ingratiated him immediately with the crew, and his knowledge of military affairs and his organizational skills ensured their continued efficient operation.

18

—— ✕ ———— ✕ ——

BETRAYED

As Winfrey and Crosson were taking on their new duties, one of the most fascinating and troubling POW camp stories of the war came to a close. It had begun three years earlier, in 1941, when Romanian general Ion Antonescu, aided by the Fascist Iron Guard, deposed King Carol II, and Romania entered the war on the Axis side. Romania showed little enthusiasm for an alliance with Germany but was eager to oppose Russia and allowed itself to be lightly occupied by German troops. As a consequence, the rich Ploieşti oil fields and refineries fell into German hands and became a critical element in keeping the Third Reich's blitzkrieg rolling.

Meanwhile, as the Allies were stabilizing the fighting in North Africa, the U.S. Twelfth Air Force at Bengazi began to expand its bombing missions and on August 1, 1943, mounted a major raid on the Ploieşti oil fields. First Lieutenant Albert M. Aronson was a twenty-eight-year-old three-year veteran at the time, flying as a navigator in a B-24 with the 415th Bombardier Squadron, Ninety-eighth Bombardier Group. Stationed at Bengazi since May 1943, he had been briefed by an MIS-X briefer, who had also taught him a secret letter code and instructed that, if captured, he was to identify himself as a CU to the senior Allied officer.[1] Complications during the raid into Romania were not expected, however, as air force officials believed the fields would be lightly defended.

Aronson and the rest of the squadron took off as scheduled, and the flight was uneventful until they reached the target, where they were surprised by heavy ground fire from antiaircraft batteries. Because the mission was a long-range one, the bombers were unaccompanied by fighter planes and were vulnerable to fire. Aronson's plane was hit, and the electrical power systems were destroyed. Flown under auxiliary power, the plane was kept under control, and its target was successfully bombed. But the right wing soon caught fire, and the number one engine was lost. The pilot, First Lieutenant Theodore Helin, made a crash landing in a cornfield.

All members of the crew managed to escape the burning aircraft but were immediately captured by Romanian soldiers and taken by truck to a German barracks in Ploieşti. Soon forty other American airmen from the raid were brought in to join them, and the combined group was fed only soup and black bread while held under German control.

The Germans were eager to move the prisoners to the Reich, but the Romanian princess Caterina Caradja, noted for her pro-Allied sympathies, warned the Germans that if the Americans were taken out of Romania, she would leave the country and go to England. As it was important to the Germans that the princess remain in the country to calm the populace, they relinquished custody of the Americans.

The Romanians, unfamiliar with POWs, interrogated the Americans individually through an interpreter and then gave them food and treated them well. The POWs were then moved to the Central School at Bucharest, until permanent quarters could be arranged at Timisul de Jos, 12 kilometers (about 7 miles) from Basou and 150 kilometers (about 93 miles) from Bucharest.

When the airmen were moved to the camp a week later, Aronson reported to Major Y, the SAO. Aronson told the major that he was familiar with a letter code that could be used to communicate with the War Department. Y thanked him, saying that he would use Aronson if he ever had anything to communicate, and then never mentioned the subject to Aronson again. So Aronson kept to himself.[2]

At the same time, Captain Wallace C. Taylor, a pilot in the 344th Bombardier Squadron, Ninety-eighth Bombardier Group, also came to Timisul de Jos. Taylor, also a CU, had been on the Ploieşti raid and had also been shot down. When he reported to Major Y, he was informed that the major, as SAO, was not interested in being consulted about messages being sent out. Y also informed Taylor that Lieutenant Aronson was in the camp and was also a CU.[3]

Taylor and Aronson met and decided between themselves to make contact under their own authority. They sent off a coded letter that MIS-X ultimately received, advising that they were POWs at Timisul.

Since Aronson had not been briefed to expect answers to his letters, he was unaware that a letter that he received shortly thereafter from Hyman Green was in fact a coded reply to his signal. He read the letter, thinking it was probably from someone he had known in school. Then Taylor also received a letter from someone he could not remember, and Aronson received a second letter from Hyman Green. Aronson now suspected that perhaps a code was being used in these letters. Having kept the first letter, he reread it and found the coded message, exclaiming to himself, "This is one of the most exciting moments of my life!"[4]

The realization that he was in direct contact with the War Department boosted his sagging morale tremendously. No longer would he feel alone in a hostile world.

But as Aronson and Taylor's morale was lifting, the rest of the camp personnel sunk into deeper depression, as the SAO began drinking and keeping company with the Romanian commandant. To counteract this, Aronson and Taylor began working more earnestly together. Using Taylor's room, they decoded the covert messages and planned their activities. Aronson was camp mess officer and had a key to the pantry, so they decided that he should be responsible for hiding the E&E material that they were starting to receive. Compasses, files, and other items were hidden in boxes of cereal, flour, and other sundries.

As E&E material began to increase, the prisoners began plotting escape, working independently at first and digging tunnels in various sections of the camp. Pickaxes and shovels were obtained from the guards in exchange for candy and cigarettes. But as the tunnels neared completion, guards would invariably arrive on the scene and destroy them. One such tunnel was dug beyond the barbed wire, but before the POWs could use it, the Romanians moved a sentry box to the exact spot where the tunnel was to exit. Someone was obviously informing the camp command that escape activities were under way.

In June 1944 Taylor and Aronson discovered something that devastated them. The officers of the camp were planning a mass escape by cutting an unguarded section of fence using a set of wire cutters sent in an MIS-X parcel. The plan was thwarted, however, when Major Y revealed the plan to the commandant. Taylor dispatched a coded letter that read: "SAO drunk PD Talked PD Escape ruined PD Plans continue PD."[5]

Winfrey went into immediate action, sending a reply through the BBC, to which he knew the POWs listened nightly, telling the Americans that they should obey the orders of United Kingdom secret agent Joseph Chanani, who had been a POW in Timisul since February 1944. Aronson knew Chanani and had in fact suspected that he might be someone special.

Aronson and Taylor contacted Chanani, who was pleased to learn that they were CUs. He then told them that he was an agent with MI-9 and had been attached to "A Force" in North Africa with Flying Officer Gideon Jacobson, also a POW at Timisul. Chanani told how he and Jacobson had parachuted into Romania and were captured while assisting the underground forces.

Taylor and Aronson were surprised to learn that the two Britishers had their own codes and could send and receive lengthy messages in a very short time through undisclosed means outside the camp.

Chanani, Jacobson, Taylor, and Aronson now formed an escape committee and began excavating tunnels. Chanani was able to get some pickaxes and shovels from guards who had been "tamed" to accept bribes. They organized a security unit to attempt to prevent leaks and find stool pigeons, and through an incredible display of ingenuity and painstaking patience, they eventually completed a long tunnel that exited beyond the wire.

They created an elaborate system of electrical wiring and constructed an air tube made of food cans from Red Cross parcels to carry oxygen down to the tunnelers. The dirt that collected from the digging was disposed of by carrying it in old suitcases that the POWs found in an unused storeroom and putting it in the attic of another unused building. For some curious reason, even though the guards saw the POWs walking around with suitcases, they never stopped them or inquired.

But despite their attempts to maintain secrecy, the escape plots continually seemed to be leaked. On the first moonless night after the tunnel was completed, eight men escaped through the tunnel. Six of the eight were recaptured immediately. Two reached Constanta on the Black Sea coast, where they were picked up by German military police and returned to the camp.

In May three POWs cut a hole through the barbed wire, intending to hide in the mountains and establish a station from which contact could be made to assist other escapees. One got away, one was caught about two hundred yards beyond the wire, and the third man was nailed as he was crawling through the fence. The escapee was picked up on a train three days later and was returned to camp, where he was beaten with rifle butts by the Romanian guards.

In July three other POWs concealed themselves in the basement of the main building of the camp. They too had planned to break out by cutting the wire in an unguarded section of the fence, but a sudden air raid alarm brought a guard to their hiding place, as if he were looking for them.

At midnight on August 24, the POWs were gathered around listening to a BBC broadcast. Suddenly, the nightly messages to the underground were interrupted, and the announcer asked listeners to stand by for a special message. Seconds later, King Carol II was broadcasting to the world that Romania had capitulated and was now on the side of the Allies. POWs in camps across Romania were subsequently advised by radio to stay put, as planes would be sent in to lift them out.

By the time Captain Taylor and Lieutenant Aronson left the camp, they had, acting almost entirely on their own, sent out sixteen coded letters, which were received and acted upon by MIS-X. In return, they had received food, clothing, and recreational parcels, a substantial amount of E&E material, and large sums of money that they were able to use to buy extra food in order to supplement the camp's meager diet. Regrettably, they were never able to count on the support of the camp SAO. They had, instead, to overcome his suspected disclosures of camp activities to the commandant in exchange for alcohol.

When Aronson and Taylor finally walked out of the gate of the prison camp, they were greeted by a Romanian guard, who saluted and then said, "Comrade Angliskis."

19

CHRISTMAS IN STALAG 17-B

TECHNICAL SERGEANT KENNETH J. Kurtenbach of the 360th Bomb Squadron, 303d Bomb Group, was a tail gunner in a B-17 with the Eighth Air Force based in England. He was on his thirteenth mission over Germany when he was shot down over Romilly-sur-Seine, France, on December 22, 1942. After reaching the ground, he determined that he was not badly injured but was lying some distance from the wrecked plane. Undiscovered by the German soldiers at the crash scene, he managed to crawl from the area and found another crewman, Staff Sergeant Joseph Dillard, not far away. Together they oriented themselves to the land using the map in their escape kit and set a course for Dieppe.

Sleeping in haystacks and barns, they were able to secure food from friendly French farmers. Their goal was to establish contact with the French underground and secure help in returning to England. However, Frenchmen in the coastal cities of Dieppe and Calais informed Kurtenbach and Dillard that very little was known of such organizations in their area and suggested they would be more likely to find capable assistance in the larger cities. The two sergeants headed for Paris by goods trains.

When they arrived, they visited cafés and bistros and always managed to secure food. But after two weeks they were still unable to obtain any information about the French underground. They decided to try a smaller city, where they might have better luck. Buying third-class tickets, they took the night train for Lyons.

At dawn, just before reaching the Lyons station, the train was shunted into a wire-enclosed area, where the Gestapo boarded to check IDs and travel permits. Lacking identification papers and unable to escape through the surrounding wire, Kurtenbach and Dillard were arrested.

At police headquarters they were interrogated vigorously; the German secret police attempted to secure confessions from them as spies. Kurtenbach's explanation that he was an evading U.S. airman was backed up by his dog tags, but the Gestapo chose to hold the men in a secure jail while they checked their stories further and so transferred them to a military prison in Dijon. Three weeks later, following several more intense interrogations, the two were moved to a regular POW camp, Stalag VII-A, at Moosburg, Germany.[1]

The camp was a huge and dirty place, holding thousands of POWs of mixed nationalities who mingled freely during the day. Officers were quartered in an adjacent compound that was partitioned off by an eight-foot wire fence.

Kurtenbach and Dillard were depressed by the camp's chaotic conditions. The barracks were infested with lice, bedbugs, and rats. Cold-water showers were limited to one a week. Laundry facilities and medical aid were almost nonexistent, and were it not for Red Cross and private food parcels, which arrived weekly, the POWs would have starved.

Compounding the deplorable physical conditions of the prison was the lack of organization among the POWs. Each nationality simply struggled for survival. Kurtenbach and Dillard realized that, without a united front, no pressure could be applied to the camp commandant for relief from the oppressive circumstances. Rallying the four hundred Americans into a semiunified body, they held an election, and Kurtenbach was elected head of the POWs, the group's Man of Confidence. But the commandant refused to meet with Kurtenbach or any other POW to discuss camp issues.[2]

Kurtenbach then appointed Sergeant Dillard as "Big X" and instructed him to set up an escape committee. Dillard then confided to Kurtenbach that he knew the letter codes, having been briefed as a CU in England by an A-2 intelligence officer.[3] Kurtenbach was stunned and jubilant.

"Great, Joe!" he told Dillard. "I was looking for someone to teach to broaden my code net. As you know we enlisted men are authorized two letters per month. You do it, get off a message advising that we require escape aids like compasses, maps, coffee, cigarettes—and especially money!"

Two months later, the first MIS-X packages began arriving in the camp, and a camp organization was beginning to develop among the American POWs, as well as within the camp in general. British POWs were making contact with MI-9, and the French were receiving comfort packages from friends and relatives.

By September 1943, however, the air war over Germany had brought another four hundred American prisoners to the camp, which was becoming unmanageably overcrowded. All the U.S. POWs were suddenly moved to Stalag 17-B at Krems, Austria, where all enlisted airmen would be incarcerated.

Upon arriving at this camp, Kurtenbach and Dillard once again confronted disarray and despair. Stalag 17-B was sprawl of wooden shacks covering thirty acres. American NCO airmen occupied five of the ten compounds. The camp was poorly organized and dirty, with bad food; POW fights served as hourly amusement for the German guards. The commandant, Colonel Kuhn, ruled with an iron hand and was utterly unreasonable and completely disinterested in improving conditions. His insensitivity to the POWs was reinforced by Major Wenglorz, the German camp security officer, who was as negative as Colonel Kuhn. Major Fred W. Beaumont was the senior American officer in the camp, but because this was an enlisted men's camp, he was not permitted to take part in the camp's administration. He was only in the camp because he was a physician and was serving as the medical doctor.

When Kurtenbach and Dillard arrived at Stalag 17-B, they once again set out to bring some military order to a chaotic routine. They held a camp election, and Kurtenbach was again elected MOC.

Kurtenbach's first administrative duty was to curb the rampant and inflationary trading going on in the camp. POWs seeking to obtain favors, supplies, escape material, food, or any other desirable item from other POWs or the German guards were creating trading wars wherein they would outbid each other for some valued item. Kurtenbach ordered that, thereafter, trading would be conducted by a committee from each of the five compounds so as to keep prices uniform and prevent competitive infighting. He then ordered all fraternizing with the German guards halted immediately.[4]

The sudden silence and cessation of bargaining seemed to frighten the Germans, and they were more cooperative with the prisoners. Delousing began and continued regularly as needed. The food, while still poor, improved. Incoming and outgoing mail was censored more rapidly, and Red Cross parcels were distributed more frequently. The compounds were cleaned, and fighting among the POWs was held to an acceptable minimum.

Kurtenbach now turned his attention to other important matters. He had been taught a secret letter code while in London and had already dispatched his first secret letter after being elected MOC, advising the War Department of his whereabouts and conditions, and requesting instructions. He had received a reply indicating that he was to establish an escape committee and signal his needs. In addition, the message advised him that a crystal radio and receiver were en route, concealed in a shoe brush.[5]

Kurtenbach organized the four thousand POWs into four battalions of one thousand men each. Each battalion elected a man to represent it on the escape committee. Sergeant Joe Dillard was elected to chair the committee as "Big X." Sergeants William Deville and John Hughes were members-at-large. Three subcommittees were set up to handle correspondence, radio, and escape activities. Sergeants Al Hadden and John L. Susan were CUs in the correspondence section. Susan had been the first CU to identify himself to Kurtenbach. To widen the correspondence network, Kurtenbach put Susan to work organizing all other CUs in the camp and ordered him to instruct selected POWs in the letter codes. As the subcommittees became established and coded signals began to be sent, camp E&E activities increased. Red Cross food parcels arrived more regularly, next-of-kin packages came more frequently, and the radio concealed in the shoe brush sailed effortlessly past camp censors and was given to Sergeant John Wasche to hide in the hospital, where he worked with Major Beaumont. Compasses, maps, money, files, wire cutters, and pliers were hidden between walls in the barracks, in hollow table legs, and in tin cans buried in the ground.[6]

Messages announcing the arrival of special parcels carrying contraband were immediately made known to

20

———×———×———

MIS-X IN COLDITZ CASTLE

COLDITZ CASTLE WAS an awesome sight: towering gray granite walls on a rocky knoll overshadowing the small town of Colditz, twenty miles southeast of Leipzig. Four stories tall, the castle itself was capped by steep, pitched roofs and had steeples at each end that looked down on the river Mulde. Since its construction in 1014 as a hunting lodge for Saxon royalty, its occupancy had changed several times until, in 1800, its black dungeons and somber rooms served as an asylum for the insane.

In 1939 the Germans took over Colditz as a POW camp for Polish and Belgian officers, adding the British in late 1940. By 1943, small contingents of all Allied nationalities were represented, and the castle had been designated as a prison for those POWs with reputations as perpetual escapers or troublemakers.

The Germans considered the castle escape-proof, as the guards outnumbered the POWs three to one. Nevertheless, the Germans erected an eight-foot-high barbed-wire fence outside the dry moat surrounding the castle and installed eighteen sentry towers, each armed with a machine gun and searchlights. Guards on foot patrolled the outer perimeter, and sound detection equipment was planted in the ground to thwart tunneling.

But barely a day passed that the French, Dutch, Belgian, Norwegian, and British POWs did not attempt an escape. In the five and a half years that Colditz served as a prison, more than 300 escape attempts were made.[1] In 130 of those attempts, the escapers succeeded in getting past the walls. By war's end thirty men had actually made "home runs,"—more successful escapes than from any other POW camp in Europe.

Each nationality in Colditz had its own escape committee, but it was not unusual for the entire garrison to cooperate on an escape attempt. MIS-X and MI-9 sent E&E material to American and British POWs respectively, but the French received the lion's share of material as their agencies and kin were geographically closest to the camp. (While the prison was in service, only eight Americans were ever incarcerated there.)

The parcel office at Colditz was different from other POW camps in that, instead of being located in an outside *Vorlager,* it was situated in one of the interior rooms of the castle. This proved to be a great boon to the POWs, as the following story by Captain William T. Lawton, British escape committee parcel officer from August 1941 to April 1945, reveals:

> Red Cross parcels were delivered to Colditz town by railroad and loaded onto local transport for delivery to the castle by British orderlies. They were then stored in the parcel office. They were distributed as and when the Germans felt like it, and no effort was made to steal these parcels, as no contraband was ever concealed in them.
>
> Private parcels, however, were addressed to individual prisoners and contained contraband. Toward the end of the summer of 1941, private

parcels were permitted into the camp by the Germans, but not frequently. These parcels contained what could be called "comforts," i.e., games, clothes, cigarettes, chocolates, etc. Coded letters were sent by certain officers to their next of kin, asking for various items of contraband—principally escape equipment—such as hacksaws, dye, money, maps, compasses, and the like. Replies in code were sent by the next of kin, giving details of any special markings on the parcels. Even if all went well, the correspondence was a drawn-out process of four to six weeks.

The private parcels then would also arrive by train and be locally transported by British orderlies, some of whom were instructed as to what to look for, i.e., names of certain officers. If a POW had a parcel waiting for him, we notified him at the morning roll call. Then, if the parcel was suspected to contain contraband, we would enter the parcel office and remove the package, before the parcels were distributed by the Germans. We entered the office with a key we had in our possession and by diverting the sentries.

In the early days of the camp, the Germans did not have X-ray equipment available for metal objects. Later, they installed a machine. Contraband did come through successfully even in unnamed parcels until the installation of the X ray. The most common method of concealing equipment was in the heels of shoes, in backgammon boards, Monopoly games, books, toilet requisites, etc. At all times there was one officer nominated as the parcel officer whose duty it was to supervise the distribution of parcels under German command.

Those for whom packages had come went to the parcel office and stood in an orderly queue in front of two grilled hatches like those in a bank or post office. The Germans did not always keep the grille down, and this indiscretion enabled me to run away with an assortment of items when I was the duty parcel officer.

A parcel had arrived unheralded, and I was standing by when the string was cut. As the paper opened, I saw in the parcel a vast amount of Reichmarks and other nefarious objects. One's immediate reaction was to pick the parcel up and run into the castle, which I did—with the loss of a few hundred Reichmarks on the way. Within a matter of seconds, the loot was divided and hidden—and despite the Germans chasing me, none of the money was found.

In the preceding account, Captain Lawton fails to mention how he came to have a key to the parcel office. The door to that office was quite substantial and was equipped with a cruciform-type lock. With a sprinkling of engineers among them, the POWs had been successful in opening all the locked doors in the castle by making various keys from bits of metal. But a cruciform lock required a four-pronged key. This was certainly not beyond the POWs' ability, but it required more time to make.

It was obvious that the lock on the parcel office door would have to be taken to the POW quarters, where it could be dismantled and a cruciform key designed and properly fitted. Banking on German adherence to routine, the POWs trusted that the parcel room would be opened only at specific times. Diverting a guard immediately after the room was closed, the POWs removed the lock from the door, fitted a key, and returned the lock before anything was noticed.

The Germans, however, knew that unauthorized people were entering the parcel office. "Be it German or

POW, the burglaries must cease!" said Captain Reinhold Eggers, chief of German security, and he ordered an electric alarm installed that would ring a bell in the guards' quarters if anyone opened the parcel office during off hours.

But the POWs once again overcame this obstacle and continued entering the office at will, even though the alarm remained in service until the end of the war.[2]

In his book, *Colditz: The German Side,* Captain Eggers recalled, "We collected and confiscated a mass of escape material from parcels. But in many respects I am bound to admit failure, failure in some cases only suspected and never proved until after the war. There must have been something wrong with our practical arrangements. I felt there were some gaps somewhere through which information and material assistance were getting in." Here a footnote explains, "Not until I read the prisoners' books after the war did I learn of their success in bypassing our parcel alarm circuit."[3]

Eggers went on to say that the German security was not entirely incompetent and did successfully confiscate money, German military passes, civilian identification, maps, messages giving the locations of frontier posts, radio parts, compasses, dyes, and blankets with pattern marks in them for making civilian suits. So much was interdicted, in fact, that Berlin took notice and directed Eggers to emulate the idea and communicate with German POWs in Allied hands. Even the British name "Dynamites," used to identify NK parcels, was copied.

The big difference was that German Dynamites never carried escape material but only news items, propaganda, and extracts from Hitler's speeches. A secret ink was developed, and messages were written on the finest Japanese paper. These were pressed into soup cubes or packed with dried beans but were usually discovered by U.S. censors; many were read and then delivered, considered harmless. Likewise, German POW replies, written in secret ink, were read and permitted to pass.

With this small success in hand, Berlin directed Eggers to send radio parts in the German Dynamite parcels to POWs. But German radio parts were too large for concealment. So Berlin ordered all the camps in Germany to send to Colditz any miniature radio parts that had been confiscated from Allied parcels. Eggers's office was snowed under with sets of every kind, size, and shape, old and new, but no miniatures suitable for clandestine shipping were among them.

The command at Colditz could not always to be fooled or taken lightly. In 1943 Lieutenant Colonel William H. Schaefer was an American infantry officer captured in North Africa and eventually taken to Oflag 64. In early July, 1944, he accidentally bumped the shoulder of a German soldier as they passed a bulletin board. Charges were filed, and Schaefer was convicted of assaulting a member of the German forces and sentenced to death. While awaiting the outcome of his appeal to the German high command, Schaefer was transferred to Colditz for safe keeping.

Upon the recommendation of the Secretary of War Henry Stimson, MIS-X sent several parcels to Schaefer from each of the societies, as well as two NK parcels. Each was heavily loaded with escape devices, including civilian clothes, money, ration coupons, and numerous blank documents that could be used for travel or work permits or military discharge papers.

But Schaefer was kept in solitary confinement and under heavy guard and never had an opportunity to make an escape. He remained in the camp until, on April 16, 1945, he, along with Flying Officer Douglas Bader—an RAF pilot with two tin legs—witnessed Captain Eggers surrender the castle to four U.S. infantry privates from the 273d Infantry of the Sixty-ninth Division.

Captain John M. Bennett, POW, Stalag Luft III, made compasses out of phonograph records. *(USAFA Library)*

One-inch-wide compass made from a phonograph record. *(Wright-Patterson Air Force Museum, Dayton, Ohio)*

Camera sent by MIS-X to Stalag Luft III; used by POWs to create forged IDs. *(Wright-Patterson Air Force Museum, Dayton, Ohio)*

Sketch of a hidey-hole in a barracks wall, where POWs hid escape contraband sent by MIS-X. *(USAFA Library)*

Technical Sergeant Kenneth Kurtenbach, Man of Confidence at Stalag 17-B, at the window of his barracks. The camera used to make this photo was one of four sent to him by MIS-X. *(Ken Kurtenbach)*

Printing press used by POWs to create travel passes and work permits. A toothbrush was used to apply ink to the type. The press was sent in pieces by MIS-X. *(R. W. Kimball)*

The parcel cart used to haul parcels from the Sagan rail depot to Stalag Luft III. *(American Red Cross)*

Three of the earliest American POWs in Germany: Buck Ingram, Lieutenant Colonel Albert P. Clark, Jr., and Ed Tourga in Stalag Luft III, 10 December 1942. *(USAFA Library)*

The U.S. Army liberates Stalag VII-A at Moosburg, Germany. *(USAFA Library)*

An unidentified American major accepts Stalag VII-A's surrender from its German commandant. *(USAFA Library)*

General George Patton (foreground, in helmet) salutes POWs at liberation of Stalag VII-A. *(USAFA Library)*

The destruction of MIS-X records by fire in 1945. *(Silvio A. Bedini)*

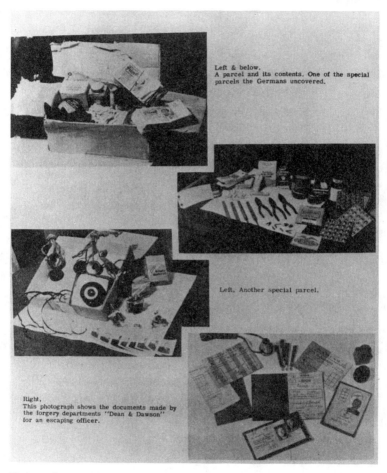

Left & below.
A parcel and its contents. One of the special parcels the Germans uncovered.

Left, Another special parcel.

Right,
This photograph shows the documents made by the forgery departments "Dean & Dawson" for an escaping officer.

Special parcels, sent by MIS-X and intercepted by German censors. Contents were money, film, developer, colored inks, files, wire cutters, button compasses, magnets, and a radio and earphones. Photo at lower right shows escape papers found by the Germans in Stalag Luft III. "Dean & Dawson" were code names used by POW forgers. *(R. W. Kimball)*

21

DELIVERANCE
FROM BERLIN

BRIGADIER GENERAL Arthur W. Vanaman was a member of the command staff of the Eighth Air Force in England on June 27, 1944. He was under orders to rotate back to the United States in three weeks for an assignment with the army air corps at Wright-Patterson Field in Dayton, Ohio.

Having never been on a bombing mission, the general requested permission to accompany a bomber before leaving England. General Carl Spaatz denied that request: Vanaman was privy to much of the Allied war strategy and, if captured, would be an ideal candidate for severe treatment by the Germans. Vanaman's desire to participate in a bombing mission was so overwhelming, however, that he disregarded Spaatz's order and found a pilot willing to take him as an observer.

Somewhere over France, flak knocked out two of the four engines in the plane, and the pilot gave the bail-out order, which was honored by most of the crew and the general. Ironically, the pilot, copilot, and flight engineer remained aboard and were able to bring the plane to a safe landing back in England.[1]

General Vanaman landed without injury but was immediately taken prisoner and—realizing Spaatz's greatest fear—became the highest-ranking American POW in Germany. Reichsmarshall Hermann Göring, upon hearing of Vanaman's apprehension, offered the general a comfortable apartment in Berlin in which to sit out the war. But the general declined the offer and was assigned to the air officers' camp at Stalag Luft III in Sagan.

The POW camp had by now grown into five compounds and held a total of fifteen thousand British and American air officers. Four of the compounds were named after the four points on the compass (North, East, South, West). The fifth, which was situated in the middle of the camp, was named Center Compound and was commanded by Colonel Delmar T. Spivey, compound SAO. General Vanaman was placed in Center Compound with Spivey.

Colonel Spivey had been the gunnery training officer at Maxwell Air Force Base in 1943. The Eighth Air Force, flying missions over Germany, was losing planes at an excessive rate, and the colonel had been assigned the task of correcting the problem. To do this, he advised the air corps that he would have to fly on several of the actual bombing missions to identify the problem. Reluctantly, the command permitted him temporary duty in England to fly five missions.[2]

Spivey had made a run over Schweinfurt without incident and had determined that the air gunners were ignoring their gunsights and were simply following the trajectory of their rounds. The bullets, flying through the air, would lose momentum and, like water coming out of a hose, would curve down before reaching the German fighter planes.

On his second mission over the Ruhr Valley, flak hit two engines, requiring the pilot to make a forced landing on the Dutch-German border. Spivey was taken prisoner and assigned to Center Compound at Stalag Luft III.

Colonel Spivey, a very compassionate man, keenly felt the plight of the POWs over which he had command and frequently went eyeball to eyeball with the German commandant to ensure his men their rights under the Geneva Convention. He also willingly gave his full attention to aiding and abetting his men's escape efforts.

Spivey's escape committee included Colonel William L. Kennedy, Captain M. E. Jackson, and Lieutenant T. E. Milligan. When Spivey asked them how to get the greatest number of men out of the camp in the shortest period of time, they replied, "Tunnel." Spivey, mindful of the ill-fated "Great Escape," nevertheless approved a plan for a four-hundred-foot tunnel to pass under the double fence of the compound and exit at the edge of a pine thicket. He then disassociated himself from the committee and appointed Colonel Kennedy to be the "Big X."[3]

Using a German-lettered typewriter that MIS-X had sent into Center Compound in several NK parcels, the POWs started typing passes and IDs for the planned escape. CU John E. Dunn, a navy lieutenant, wrote a coded letter requesting civilian clothing, and the men on the escape team began to dig.

The tunnel was code-named "George" and began in the false bottom of a cooking stove in Barracks One. The concrete base beneath the stove had been hollowed out, and the range rested on the four corners of the hole. It could be slid over far enough to allow the diggers to excavate, and they dug twenty-five feet deep before starting the four-hundred-foot-long lateral escape tunnel. The dirt was hauled up by a rope in gallon cans to the sixty "penguins," who then walked a meandering route through the camp that would always take them to the playing fields and a ball game. Pulling a string in their pockets, the penguins would release the dirt from a pouch inside their trousers, and the dirt would then be trampled into the ground by the ball players.

Over one hundred POWs were posted as lookouts with orders to call "Tally-ho" if a German came within 100 feet of the barracks. Another twenty-five men formed an inner security circle to intercept and detain any German who eluded the first defense and came within twenty-five feet of the digging. The POWs would request a match, ask a question, or even stage a fight—do anything they could—to delay the guard the few seconds that were required to "button up" the tunnel before a "goon" gained entry to the barracks.[4]

While the digging continued, Lieutenant David Bowling, who spoke German well, was selected to make a one-man escape to carry a very important message from General Vanaman to the War Department. Rumors carried by the guards, civilian workmen in the camp, and newly arriving POWs indicated that the war was turning drastically against the Germans, and they were beginning to consider POWs a liability to the Third Reich. Himmler was publicly advocating mass execution of the POWs by the SS as a solution. General Vanaman wanted to know the War Department's policy if Hitler granted Himmler control of the camps and the POWs were in danger.

Lieutenant Bowling was supplied with civilian clothes, money, train schedules, a compass, a new pair of wire cutters, and an ID as a French laborer being transferred. Sleeping under the barracks, Bowling was to wait for the camp to settle down for the night and then crawl to the wire, cut through, and head for the rail depot at Sagan one mile away, where he could catch the early morning train.

As lights-out was sounded at 2200 hours, word was passed throughout the barracks that an escape was to be attempted and that the POWs were to stall in responding to any roll calls, delaying the count to give the escaper time to clear the area.

Sleep came to only a few that night as memories of

the "Great Escape" were relived. The POWs heard the changing of the guard at midnight, and no alarm sounded. At around 0145 hours, the POWs heard shouting, but it soon died down, and no roll call was taken that night. The next morning, Bowling's absence was covered up and speculation ran high that perhaps he had made it. Only a few would ever know a few months later that Bowling had actually succeeded in making a home run.[5]

In the meantime, the tunnel was all but completed within six weeks, leaving only the final three feet to break through. Two men were selected to make the initial exit, but after traveling three hundred feet through the tunnel, they panicked and returned to the barracks. Their escape material was collected, and a new attempt was scheduled forty-eight hours later.

But the next morning the POWs were held at roll call as dozens of special ferrets entered the compound and discovered "George" within an hour. An inside informer was immediately suspected by the angry POWs, but a culprit was never determined.

After this failed attempt, the focus of the escape committee shifted from escape to self-defense in the camp. The Russian army was advancing on Germany and the end of the war seemed in sight. Rumors were growing stronger that Himmler and the SS would indeed gain control of the prison camps and execute the POWs.

To coordinate their survival efforts, the POWs in the different compounds began communicating with each other by placing a message in a rock-filled tin can and throwing it over the barbed wire that separated the compounds. In one such "correspondence," Colonel Spivey received word from Colonel Goodrich that South Compound had received a radio transmitter in a hot parcel. The radio had not yet been tried out, and Goodrich wanted Spivey's suggestions. The set was described as a fifteen-watt unit, operating on a low-band frequency. Air force radio men in the camp had indicated that, if a transmitted signal from this set "skipped," it could reach London. Spivey told Goodrich not to risk discovery of the radio but to hold it in readiness in the event some emergency situation arose. In the meantime, the POWs would continue trying to obtain any information they could on the future of the camps.

For this purpose, Colonel Kennedy appointed Lieutenant W. W. Brown as his agent, through whom all information would be passed. Lieutenant Brown had a staff of French- and German-speaking POWs whose job it was to sound out German guards and workmen as well as French laborers working in the camp. To prevent two of the staff from asking the same German the same leading question and arousing suspicion, each member of Brown's staff was eventually assigned to a specific guard.[6]

After every camp search for contraband by the Germans, Colonel Kennedy would privately meet with Brown to determine if the Germans had any particular reason for conducting the search. Guarding against leaks by stool pigeons was more important now than ever, and the Germans never gave up attempting to place a spy among the POWs.

Lieutenant Brown's team began to prove its worth as information began to trickle in suggesting that the Germans would attempt to evacuate the camp in late January. All personnel were directed to begin saving food, mending clothing, and creating packs to carry their belongings. In addition, Spivey ordered every man to hike at least four miles daily around the camp to get into condition.

On January 27, 1945, at about 2100 hours, a member of the German staff came into the camp and ordered the POWs to be ready to evacuate in thirty minutes. The Russians were twenty-five kilometers (about sixteen miles) to the east, and the Germans wanted to prevent them from liberating the American and British POWs.

Ten inches of snow blanketed the ground, and the temperature stood between one and ten degrees Fahrenheit.

As the two thousand POWs in South Compound formed up, the tower guards turned on the lights, giving the area the appearance of an anthill as POWs scurried about digging up their hidden food in the frozen ground. Camp history sheets were distributed among five hundred trustworthy men, who hid the papers in the linings of their coats, trousers, caps, or shoes.[7]

At 0300 hours on January 28, the first block of two thousand airmen from Center Compound marched out through the front gate of Stalag Luft III to begin the grueling 100-mile trek to Spremberg, where they would then be loaded into boxcars for the remaining 350-mile journey to Moosburg. Brigadier General Vanaman and Colonel Spivey stepped to the head of the long column and began trudging southwest.

Each man was issued a Red Cross food parcel as he exited the gate, but three days later they were down to the food bits that Spivey had directed them to collect. The Germans clearly had made no prior arrangements for housing or feeding the POWs. As they marched through the countryside, however, the POWs were often able to trade cigarettes for vegetables from German civilians who came out of their homes to watch the column pass by.[8]

Sleeping in the open, in barns, churches, and theaters each night, the men were permitted to make fires only to heat water. Any food was, by Spivey's order, to be shared: if a few cans of Spam or corned beef were available, the food was to be cubed and placed in a communal pot.

On the afternoon of February 5, the POWs entered Spremberg, where General Vanaman and Colonel

Spivey were ordered to accompany a German officer to Berlin for immediate repatriation. Spivey noted in his diary, "I was an angry man that day as I stood on the sidewalk and watched my men march by to the rail cars. I wanted to curse and kill every German in sight and take my men and go home." He insisted on waiting until all two thousand POWs were aboard the boxcars before he consented to join the German officer who would take him and the general to Berlin.

When they reached the German capital, Spivey's diary continues,

> [The city] was a shambles. Instead of there being moving traffic, there were scurrying feet. The train to take us to another station across town was not running, so we walked. There were dead horses still harnessed to overturned wagons, streetcars blocked intersections, buildings burned, and on all sides we heard the crash as brick walls collapsed. Moans, cries, and yells mixed with grotesque shadows accentuated by the flames, leaving a Dante's Inferno. Finally, arriving at the other depot, we found our other train for Luckenwalde.[9]

Vanaman and Spivey ultimately reached their destination and were assigned to a Polish officers' quarters in another POW camp, where "even the German commandant never knew why we were brought there." Days passed, until word came that there had been a change of plans, and the two officers were moved into a German army barracks. More days passed uneventfully.

Colonel Spivey knew that the war-ravaged transport system in Germany prevented little if any food and medical supplies from reaching the camps, and the safety of his men still worried him. He and Vanaman each sent letters appealing to the German high command to deal with the POWs' pressing needs. Word eventually came back that American army trucks, driven by Canadian POWs on parole, would depart from Switzerland with food and medicine for the camp POWs. General Gottlob Berger, supreme German commandant of POWs, guaranteed that the convoys would receive safe passage to the now nearly forty thousand Allied POWs who were being held at Stalag VII-A in Moosburg, Germany. Male members of the International Red Cross from Switzerland were to ride in the cab of each truck to ensure safe arrival.

When they heard that the relief supplies had arrived safely at the camp, General Vanaman and Colonel Spivey next pressed for an explanation for their detention in Berlin. General Berger responded with an extraordinary request. He and other high-ranking officers were ready to assassinate Hitler, who they said was insane, and surrender to the British and American forces—if the United States and Britain would join Germany to fight the Russians. Berger proposed that General Vanaman and Colonel Spivey take a letter from him back to the Americans that would outline a code the American army could use to contact the SS by radio if it approved of his plan.

"Both General Vanaman and I," Spivey's diary records, "made it clear we could not guarantee any reaction on the part of the United States government." They did, however, agree to deliver Berger's message, on the condition that the Germans continue to grant safe passage to the International Red Cross serving the POWs and that the POWs not be moved again regardless of Allied advances.

Berger agreed and also promised that the officers would not be held responsible for anything beyond delivering the letter. "German radio will be listening for any message the U.S. forces would broadcast as a result of the code enclosed," he told Spivey and Vanaman.[10]

Early in the morning, General Vanaman and Colonel Spivey set out for Switzerland in a small German staff car driven by Lieutenant Otto Werther, who was carrying papers signed by General Berger allowing the party to pass German lines without question. Their biggest risk, however, was now from Allied fighter planes that might strafe them. "It was a harrowing ride, taking three days," Spivey wrote in his diary, "but we finally reached a river about 200 yards wide separating Germany from Switzerland. The guards stood at attention as we approached and drove slowly across the bridge onto Swiss soil."

The officers were then driven to Zurich, where they met with the American consul. General Vanaman produced the secret letter from the hollow of his heel, and the consul dispatched it to Washington by radio. Vanaman was flown to America, where he reported to the War Department, and Spivey went to Reims, France, where he reported to General Spaatz.

Nothing was done about the offer of surrender, and the reply code was not used. Germany was so close to defeat that a fractional surrender would have not been viable.

Spivey later received an explanation as to why he and General Vanaman had spent so many weeks waiting for repatriation. Hitler had been so angered by the American bombing of Dresden that he had ordered General Berger to kill all American POWs. Berger ignored the order, and in the confusion of the final days of the Third Reich, Hitler never checked to see if it had been carried out. Berger then personally transported several hundred French, British, American, and Polish diplomatic prisoners across the Swiss border.

At the Nürnberg trials, General Berger was tried and sentenced to twenty-five years by the War Tribunal. He was, however, given a full pardon after serving six years, owing to testimony on his behalf given by General Vanaman and Colonel Spivey.[11]

22

✗ ✗

ORDERED DESTROYED

THE WIND IN late October 1944 rattled the twin freight doors at 1142 noisily, causing Peterson to look up from his work. He and Hitchcock had just completed stuffing the last of the sixty parcels that now covered the long shipping counter. Stepping back, he looked at Major Crosson, who, clipboard in hand, made the final check of his penciled figures.

"It all tallies right, Sergeant," Crosson said to Peterson. "You can seal them up. Incidentally, this will be the last shipment of escape devices—unless we receive an unexpected order down the line. The camp SAOs are reporting very few losses of material and their inventories are up. The Pentagon thinks that the war will be over by Christmas."

Hitchcock, happy-go-lucky as always, broke into "California Here I Come," but Peterson was more restrained. "Don't start that yet, Maurice," he cautioned. "Until it happens, Uncle Sam still owns you. Besides, there's still Japan to consider."

Two hours later, the two men finished wrapping and labeling the parcels, stuffed them into mailbags, locked the pouches, and inserted the coded address cards into the routing clips. The process had become second nature by now. For the past eleven weeks, they had been pushing out three hundred loaded packages a week, along with an equal number of straight food boxes.

The next morning, Shoemaker loaded the sixty parcels on his truck and reported to Major Crosson that he was ready to depart for Baltimore.

"Well, Shoemaker," the major said, "we may not be sending any more parcels, but you will continue to make one trip each week to the post office. The Servicemen's Relief still has a p.o. box there for its general address, and we will have to continue monitoring the box for mail. Every so often, a POW who receives a package from the organization sends a thank-you letter. I'd also like you to spot-check the Ben Franklin store in Baltimore while you're in town. I've already advised our collaborating manufacturers to hold up all further loading of their products, but I want you to make sure that nothing accidentally slips through."

Shoemaker acknowledged that he would keep an eye out for letters and errant shipments and then left for his post office run.

The weeks then began to drag by. There was no work to do, but the men were still required to be on hand. Few coded messages requesting supplies were coming over to the Warehouse, as the camps were stocked. All organized escape committees had radios by now, so most correspondence was being transmitted through coded BBC broadcasts rather than MIS-X mail.

At Christmas the crews of the Creamery and Warehouse were granted a seven-day leave, and Shoemaker moved into the Warehouse as a temporary security guard. Though the winter was typically cold, the building was finally heated, as the reduction in production and thus flammable solvents permitted Crosson to authorize installation of a stove in the shop, where the only chimney was located.

Inactivity continued into the new year. By February 1945, the anticipated end of the war was becoming more believable, as reports from the front of camp liberations were received.

In February a courier arrived from the Pentagon with a report for Major Crosson. Prepared by a Swiss representative of the International Red Cross, the memo gave the following figures of POWs evacuated from camps in front of the advancing Russian army:

Prison Camp	POWs Liberated
Oflag 64, Schubin	1,444
Stalag Luft III, Sagan	6,765
Stalag 344, Lamsdorf	108
Stalag 20-A, Thorn (Toruń)	40
Stalag II-B, Hammerstein	7,087
Stalag III-B, Fürstenburg	4,646
Stalag III-C, Alt Drewitz	2,034
Stalag Luft IV, Grosstychow	8,600[1]

But the excitement about the safety of these POWs was dimmed by apprehension concerning the remaining prisoners. Hitler had publicly threatened to kill all remaining POWs rather than liberate them. It was his final effort—his ransom against defeat.

The men at 1142 anguished over the plight of the still-captive POWs. During the previous two years, the crew had come to know the names and struggles of these men and had banded together in a covert effort to supply them with a measure of hope. With German roads and rails now in ruins, however, it was impossible for MIS-X to get any aids, food, or medical supplies to the POWs.

For the first time, MIS-X began to feel the same helplessness the POWs did.

Then, toward early March, the Allied Intelligence Services advised the Allied Supreme Command that the war would soon end and preparations should begin for receiving and debriefing approximately three hundred thousand British and American prisoners of war. MIS-X briefers were immediately brought in to help coordinate the enormous process by which the POWs would be cleared and sent home. Nothing was to be done yet, but the mechanics of the debriefing machinery were being constructed: the briefers were beginning to recruit unassigned officers in Europe to assist in handling the release of the prisoners.

On May 2, 1945, the Russians captured Berlin, and on May 8 Germany surrendered. The long-rumored end of the European war had come to pass.

Immediately, word came that the staff at 1142 should begin plans for shutting down MIS-X.

THE PERSONNEL AT FORT Hunt celebrated the end of the war with the rest of the world. The post commander, Colonel John Walker, ordered martial music played on the P.A. system, and everyone except the duty men converged on the parade ground for soda-pop, hot dogs, and baseball.

But work remained to be done. Special agents of MIS-X sought out the SAOs and escape committee members from the various camps, to be processed first and then flown to Washington for detailed debriefing while their memories on camp E&E activities were still clear. Briefers gathered with their crews at Camp Lucky Strike in Reims, France, where POWs poured through twenty-four hours a day, and hospitals, supply rooms, and mess halls were busy around the clock.

Major Crosson and either Captain Churchill or Sergeant Bedini from the Creamery were making frequent trips to the Pentagon to attend briefings on their activities in MIS-X. But the remainder of the technical and correspondence crews continued to sit out the closing days at 1142, idle and impatient.

Toward the end of June, as most of the technical section was gathered around a large map of Asia listening to Major Crosson discuss the war's progress in the Pacific, Sergeant Peterson asked the question that had long been on everyone's mind: "Major, what ever happened to Colonel Winfrey and the two million dollars?"

"I don't know," the major replied. "The Pentagon has had a couple of memos from him, but last I heard he was in China trying to set up some native food vendors to carry fresh vegetables into the camps in China. You know those baskets that coolies carry across their shoulders on bamboo poles? Well, someone thought to hollow the bottoms out, and our fellows are putting money and medicine in there. The coolies load up the baskets with food and then go to the camps. POWs are paid twenty cents a day by the Japanese, and the natives are allowed to enter the camps. So the prisoners can purchase fresh produce and get the secret supplies. But that's about all that we can do, as the Japanese are very strict about the number of parcels they allow to be shipped into their camps."

It was not a hopeful note, and Major Crosson paused for a moment.

"It's hard to say where Winfrey is, or what he's doing," the major continued. "Communications with the States is so difficult. Admiral Nimitz has authorized his naval units to pass MIS-X traffic back to us. But General MacArthur commands the army and air forces—and his policy is to allow no intelligence personnel or operations in his theater unless he has command over them. As a consequence, in MacArthur's Pacific theater, MIS-X loses its identity and becomes only a cog in the big wheel known as AIB, or Allied Intelligence Bureau—which is MacArthur's intelligence operation.

"Most combat troops are briefed before going overseas, and our job is basically to design and issue the escape and survival kits that are given to the airmen—be they army or navy—who are fighting over the jungle or ocean. Once an airman is down and his location is known, we coordinate his rescue. We have, however, no personnel to draw on—and we don't even have any equipment. So we borrow personnel from the army or navy, and our people lead the rescue parties. We don't hear much about what happens, as the records go through MacArthur's HQ and end up in Canberra."

The major was called away to the phone, and that was the last the crew ever heard of MIS-X activities or Colonel Winfrey in the Pacific theater.

ON AUGUST 14, JAPAN surrendered, and World War II was finally over on all fronts. The staffs of the technical and correspondence sections had completed their preliminary shut-down tasks, and now awaited the mustering-out procedure so they could go home.

Six days later, Major Crosson, waiting for orders to bring MIS-X to a close, received the phone call he was awaiting but not the message. "Burn all your records," Colonel Catesby ap Jones instructed him from the Pentagon, "and all artifacts on hand, within the next twenty-four hours."

Colonel ap Jones then informed the major that an officer had to be present at all times to supervise the activity and certify its completion in writing. "And major," the colonel concluded, "I realize that this is an unusual order, so I am sending a courier over with a copy of it in writing."

Major Crosson called the crew together and told them of this unexpected order. "I'm not sure how we'll do this," he confided to the men. "We have no facilities for incineration. But we're going to be real busy very soon, so I recommend that you go to the mess, now.''

Major Crosson then called the post commander, Colonel Walker, for suggestions. The colonel said that the fires could probably be contained in thirty-gallon GI garbage cans, which he would have the post maintenance crew deliver.

At about 11:30 A.M., ap Jones's courier arrived from the Pentagon, and the post maintenance truck pulled up with three new steel garbage cans and some stones on which to set the cans. For ventilation and to aid in the burning, holes had been cut into the bottoms of the cans with an axe.

Lieutenant McTighe was appointed to oversee the destruction of MIS-X materials, and the shirtless crew began carrying out file drawers of supplies. No evidence was to remain. Loaded games and items were broken and their contents removed to ensure that both were actually destroyed in the fire. Wires from radios were cut into pieces. In the sweltering heat, the men stirred the flames and burned everything they had created. Meal breaks were staggered so there was never a time when the burning was halted or left unattended. Papers were wadded up to ensure that they would be burned and not simply scorched. For thirty-six straight hours, through the unbearably humid day and night, the records and E&E devices of MIS-X were incinerated.

Crosson's next order was to dispose of the remaining usable inventory in the Warehouse. The Salvation Army was called and removed all the food items; Walter Reed Hospital was invited to pick up the straight game boards, cards, and clothes. But items still remained—among them the one-ton printing press, the paper cutter, and printer's type. Watching the truck arrive from Walter Reed, Crosson decided to give the hospital the remaining blankets, sheets, and razors. "Get your men started," he told the young lieutenant, who had come with the five men in the truck. "It all goes."

Then, realizing what he had said, Crosson quickly excused himself. "I'll be right back!" he said with a mischievous smile on his face.

Hurrying to his office, Crosson removed the last page of the inventory list. Giving it to his clerk, he said, "Quick, Huss, add on the press, paper cutter, type, inks, and paper. Also, all the other hand tools. This young officer is going to sign for this stuff and won't even know the difference."

And with that, MIS-X was shut down.

Its activities have remained a mystery to this day. And, even after the writing of this book, many questions remain. Among the most treasured to the men who worked in the Warehouse is: What did Walter Reed Hospital ever do with the one-ton printing press?

AFTERWORD

I FIRST LEARNED THAT MIS-X had surfaced publicly when I read a 1984 newspaper item describing the celebration by the John Waddington Company of Leeds, England, on their fiftieth anniversary of manufacturing Monopoly. The article told how the game board had been used by British intelligence (MI-9) during World War II as a carrier for escape aids to POWs. Mentioned in the article was Professor M. R. D. Foot, a former senior British intelligence officer and author of the book *MI-9*.

I had maintained my own silence for forty years, never once mentioning or even hinting of MIS-X's activities to anyone. Though my part in MIS-X was limited, I was quite well versed on the operation. I was eager to know if MI-9 had been declassified and if Foot made any mention of MIS-X in his book. A copy of *MI-9* seemed the best place to start. Not finding a copy in the leading bookstores or libraries, I obtained Professor Foot's number and telephoned him in London.

He did indeed have a copy and promised to mail me one. He was delighted to learn I had been with MIS-X and asked if I intended to write a book. The idea had occurred to me, so I asked if he thought the idea feasible.

"Indeed I do," he responded emphatically. "Not only feasible, it definitely should be done. But please remember, you must be very sure of your facts and give confirmation right down the line."

I next telephoned the National Archives in Washington, D.C., who confirmed they did indeed hold records related to MIS-X. These collections were open to the public, and the archivist explained the procedure to gain access.

Upon arrival at the Washington National Record Center, Richard Boylan, military archivist, had a large four-wheeled freight truck trundled into the study room. I was amazed at the volume of material he was offering and realized it would require several days to view it all, even with my researcher's assistance.

Boylan informed me, "I doubt you will garner too much from it all, as the combers have been through it three times. In cataloging we could not tell what MIS-X was, or what they did." When I advised him that I had been a member of the group, he appeared surprised and circumspectly asked me several questions. My replies were concise but sufficient for him to be convinced of my claim.

As Steven J. Ovens, my researcher, and I shuffled through several thousand documents over a five-day period, it became obvious that the files contained only bits and pieces of disconnected reports. Most of the files had no cover page to identify the originator, subject, or date. They would make little sense to anyone not having prior knowledge of the MIS-X operation. While I photocopied a large number of documents, each with its declassification number, the yield was very disappointing considering the time and expense I had invested. The material I had would not even confirm, much less disclose in detail, the exploits of MIS-X; I would have to look elsewhere.

The next place to turn was the U.S. Army History Center in the Pulaski Building in Washington. My telephone call was referred to Dr. Brooks Kleber, the assistant chief historian. He was guardedly helpful, assuring me the center held no MIS-X material, and asked how I had learned of the unit. My answer clearly surprised him, and after we talked for several minutes, he said he had been a POW at Oflag 64.

Within a week the copy of *MI-9* arrived via air mail from London, and I dived in, hoping to relive the secrets of over forty years ago. But Foot's book touched only lightly on MIS-X, and I would not be able to use it as my confirmation. Some footnotes, however, indicated that helpful references could be found at the Air Library at Maxwell Air Force Base. I went to Montgomery, Alabama, where the Air Library supplied hundreds of documents I selected from their card-file index. Some rich material was found mingled with unrelated files, but none carried a notice of declassification. Nevertheless I was assured that anything available to me was a public file.

I moved on to the Office of Air Force History at Bolling Field Air Force Base in Maryland, which had been mentioned at the Air Library. I found it to be a modern, updated library using microfilm. This facilitated much more rapid research and enabled me to collect a large number of papers relevant to my quest.

While having lunch in Washington, I remembered that Silvio A. Bedini had been our cryptoanalyst at 1142. I had heard that he worked at the Smithsonian Institution. If he could be located, I thought he might offer some assistance. His name jumped out at me as I scanned the phone book on a whim, and within minutes we were renewing our acquaintance. He was delighted to hear from me after so many years and offered to extend all possible assistance.

"Go see Colonel Winfrey," he said. "He lives in Arlington, just across the river." I was reluctant to leave Silvio hanging, but my plane left in six hours for the West Coast. "See Winfrey," he urged, "We can get in touch any time later on." I found Winfrey's number and dialed. It was exciting to hear his voice, and I quickly identified myself, expecting to hear his enthusiastic response. Instead, there were some long pauses as I refreshed his memory on our service together at Fort Hunt. Finally he agreed to see me at his home, and a taxi brought me to his front door a half-hour later.

Age had caught up with him. His eyes were failing, and his recollection about certain details of the past were somewhat unclear. He did not remember me or my name. We talked for better than an hour. On some issues he was quite lucid, but he gradually shifted the topic to the trials he had at sea after being torpedoed when trying to reach England early in the war.

He remembered 1142 well, but he recalled nothing about the little black truck we had used. From Fort Hunt in August 1944, he remembered having gone to his next assignment, in China. But here his mind faltered again and the details escaped him. At my mention of the two million dollars he had been escorting, he perked up. "I only had time to disburse half of it when the war ended, and I gave it to a major who was staying on in China." I finally left, saddened at what age had done to this exceptional man, whose razor-sharp mind had built MIS-X.

THE LIBRARY AT THE Air Force Academy turned out to be the jackpot of my quest. Here, with the contributions of the ex-POWs of Stalag Luft III, and with the guidance of Lieutenant General Albert P. Clark, Jr., and Duane Reed, archivist, the Special Collections Section has gathered thousands of papers and photographs that tell the story of U.S. airmen downed in Germany during World War II. My letter requesting an appointment was promptly answered, advising me that the Monday I had specified would coincide with Reed's schedule and that my interview with General Clark had been set up for the following day.

With my researcher in tow, I arrived on the specified Monday and was greeted warmly by Mr. Duane Reed. He had laid out for our review a display consisting of many thousands of pages of POW history and hundreds of photographs. We were only an hour into our research when General Clark entered. Having been so active in the camp escape work, he was unable to restrain himself and wait one more day for our scheduled meeting.

At seventy-two years of age his posture was still as straight as the day he had graduated from West Point in 1936. His hair was still flaming red; his handshake, as firm as a blacksmith's. "I've waited forty years to learn about MIS-X, and developed darn little, so let's talk," he said.

From that moment on, our research went splendidly. The special collections held hundreds of photographs taken in the camp with the cameras I had purchased and dispatched via MIS-X. In a three-hour session, General Clark and a colleague, Colonel John M. Bennett, detailed much of the camp escape organization and many of the exploits involved in getting the contraband escape aids into the camp. The ice had finally been broken, and the documentary confirmation of my story began to take shape. Three months later I was asked to address the 1987 Stalag Luft III Appell held in Seattle. Over six hundred ex-POWs were on hand. It was the first time that MIS-X had been spoken of publicly, and when the code users and their role was mentioned, several heads in the audience snapped up, I'm sure involuntarily. Smiles appeared on a few faces, and one member even winked at me. The *Vorlager* parcel office was of special interest to me, and I closed my talk by requesting that anyone with firsthand knowledge meet with me.

Stepping off the podium, I was inundated by newspaper reporters, all talking at once. Strobes flashed, and three television cameramen with their cumbersome video equipment fought for the best angle. The *Seattle Times* headlined the story of MIS-X on the front page of the following morning's edition, complete with my picture.

For the next six months, letters and phone calls poured in from ex-POWs around the nation. Many who had not been present at the reunion were intrigued just at hearing about MIS-X and wrote to ask questions. A few sent outlines of some incident in which they had participated at camp. Many were interesting, daring, or humorous, and they also contained names and addresses of buddies who might know something. I sent off over two hundred letters with stamped and addressed reply envelopes enclosed.

I next came in contact with General John K. Waters, a four-star general who had retired a commander-in-chief of the U.S. Army in the Pacific. He had been a code user at Oflag 64 and had sent the message requesting small-caliber guns. I felt his story would add immensely to my book and flew to Maryland for an agreed-upon interview. He, like General Clark, had tried many times during his years in the military to locate any of the technicians and mechanics of MIS-X, but to no avail. He invited me to attend the Oflag 64 ex-POW reunion coming up in October at Alexandria, Virginia. It would be my fifth flight across the nation in two years. But the reunion was a disappointment, with less than one hundred members present. "The people you want to see are all dead," John Slack, adjutant, told me. "We aren't spring chickens anymore."

Being close to Washington, I returned to talk with Dr. George Chalou at the National Archives. He had set up the Modern Military History records at Suitland,

Maryland, which included an MIS-X file. He had become very interested in the unit from the bits and pieces available but had never garnered a clear picture of what it did.

He received me graciously, taking a full hour from his busy schedule. "I have searched over twenty years for the Pentagon files on MIS-X, without success," he told me. "If you develop any information in the course of your research, I would appreciate your sharing it with me. The purpose of the archives is to preserve our history, and we lack a full picture for MIS-X."

Three months later, I encountered Colonel Harry Osterweis, who, I had learned, possibly held the key to the long trail of missing MIS-X Pentagon papers. Osterweis was one of the five original officers inducted into MIS-X in mid-1942. When I asked him about the lost MIS-X files, he responded, "Why, they aren't lost. I know where they are. In 1946 I was called back into service by Colonel Russell Sweet to help box up the Pentagon records and a number of artifacts. They were placed in wooden boxes and sent to Mitchell Air Force Base on Long Island, in New York." He paused, as if thinking, "But the base was closing down at about the time the records arrived. So, they were trans-shipped to the federal depository at Kansas City, Missouri."

Upon returning to Oregon, one of my first acts was to telephone Dr. Chalou and pass along what I had discovered.

"There is no government depository at Kansas City," Chalou said. "However, there is a large military record center at St. Louis." There was a long pause. "But it sustained a major fire in 1974 and burned to the ground. Millions of military documents were destroyed."

As of this writing, Dr. Chalou says he is no closer to locating the lost MIS-X files, and that evidence continues to point to the fire as the explanation for their disappearance. This book, then, may be the only written history of the MIS-X contribution to the war. My petition to the home secretary in London to view MI-9 records was denied, as there is no provision in British law that permits an alien to examine those British archives.

My requests to other ex-POW organizations were also denied, and I encountered reluctance to transmit my requests to their memberships. They had been deluged by salesmen seeking access to their membership rolls and were fearful of what I might do with a list of names and addresses once I was finished with it. I regret that I did not receive their cooperation, and I suspect that there is important information some of these ever-discreet veterans will carry to their graves.

Kenneth Kurtenbach, however, was located. He served as Man of Confidence at both Stalag VII-A in Moosburg and Stalag 17-B in Krems and has been generous with his time and knowledge. He put into my hands material that gave valuable insight into the activities of their escape organizations.

Some explanation is due the reader on how the artifacts shown in this book survived the 1945 destruction order. On V-J Day, Colonel Winfrey was on an island in the South Pacific. Being a senior officer not assigned to a combat unit, with the war over, he cut his own orders for immediate return to the United States. He had in his possession an army field locker that contained a variety of MIS-X items loaded with escape aids. These were classified as Most Secret/Top Secret, and they could not simply be surrendered to a field quartermaster, the way excess equipment would normally be handled.

Upon arrival stateside, Winfrey tried unsuccessfully to locate an intelligence officer with sufficient rank to be made accountable for accepting them. Winfrey could not communicate too many details to anyone. Stymied, he accepted his discharge from the service, carried the footlocker home, and placed it in his attic. For the next forty years, he told me, he wrote letters to the army trying to find someone to accept custody of the footlocker and its contents, to no avail.

Winfrey did remember Silvio Bedini and knew he worked as deputy director at the Smithsonian Institution. From Bedini he learned that certain MIS-X records had been declassified, so he offered his material to the museum.

The museum accepts over three million donations per year, and by the time I was far enough into this book to consider pictures, the artifacts had become enmeshed in government red tape. Only through the extraordinary efforts of Silvio A. Bedini were the photographs made possible.

The baseball with the radio component concealed inside was a "gift" that reached me through the mails along with an Acey-Ducey game. A single piece of paper carried the words, "From Norman. They are loaded." I am reasonably sure I know who Norman is. How he acquired the items is his secret.

The ball still carried the S-2 adhesive sticker on the horsehide outer cover, which was the code we applied to designate the contents. I wanted to confirm that the radio component capsule was indeed inside the ball and went to see my family physician, Dr. Harvey Price. He was delighted to assist me, and within five minutes I had a doctor's order for an X ray of one baseball. At the Salem Radiology Laboratory, Claudia Bennett Layton, radiologist, was perplexed at the order to X-ray a baseball, but after a brief explanation, she produced an excellent image. It distinctly reveals the oblong metal core in the center of the ball. I believe the Acey-Ducey game board is also loaded with maps and/or Reichmarks. However, I am not able to confirm it nondestructively, as an X-ray setting energetic enough to penetrate wood would be too high to distinguish any paper content.

* * *

MIS-X SERVED ALL BRANCHES of the service equally but did not dictate to the POWs how the escape aids should be employed or by whom. The Articles of War prescribed that each American POW should avail himself of the opportunity to escape, and should continue to resist and upset his captors' routine until such time as he does escape or is liberated.

Escape figures are vague and often conflicting. The best records I found, supported by the Veterans Administration, list 95,532 members of the U.S. military forces captured in the European theater during World War II. Of this number, the VA recognizes 737 men as successfully escaping to return to their commands. The VA makes no distinction between officers and enlisted personnel in these figures. A copy of the *Study of Prisoners of War* (1980) is available from the Veterans Administration.

A memo prepared by Colonel Russell Sweet to Colonel Catesby ap Jones after V-E Day itemizes an estimate of American escapers and evaders as follows:

Occupied Belgium and Germany	3,096
Occupied Holland and Denmark	47
Italian POW camps	6,335
North Africa	18
Occupied Greece	100
Albania and Yugoslavia	1,333
Japanese occupied areas	218
From China through AGAS	853
	12,000

M. R. D. Foot, in his book *MI-9*, lists the same figures but points out that they are suspiciously rounded off. They do, however, closely coincide with those of Brigadier Norman Crockatt, also of MI-9. Discrepancies exist, particularly in the Italian theater. There, Foot says, Crockatt may be two thousand short, while Sweet may be two thousand over for the American escapers and evaders.

A possible explanation for such discrepancies could be in the manner different Allied commanders classified evasions when reporting to higher authorities. An officer missing in action could pop up at a later date stating he had spent the interim evading the enemy and have his explanation generally accepted without question. An enlisted man, however, had to return to the command with an officer or have solid confirmation of his actions. Lacking such confirmation, enlisted personnel were often referred to the criminal investigators to determine whether they had been AWOL. Such a system of record building could only result in ambiguous figures.

Dr. Brooks Kleber says the U.S. Army History Center has no figures on U.S. escapers or evaders in Europe during World War II. This leaves Sweet's memo to Jones, however flawed or accurate, as the only figures from within MIS-X that I found in my research. They do appear plausible.

Finally, special mention should be made of the code users who were active in the camps. They never knew who received the coded messages they addressed to relatives or friends, but their efforts provided the War Department with a great deal of hard intelligence relayed through MIS-X. Had their actions ever been discovered by the enemy, the CUs could have been executed as spies. In recognition of the sacrifices made by these men, they were awarded the Bronze Star. But then, as this book illustrates, virtually all of the American POWs were engaged in a battle against the enemy from behind their barbed-wire front, and MIS-X helped them do it.

APPENDIX I

———— ✗ ———— ✗ ————

MIS-X and the Pacific Theater

(Author's note: Virtually nothing is known of the activities of MIS-X in the Pacific theater. Perhaps somewhere there are records that will one day come to light. Perhaps there is someone still alive who served with MIS-X in this region who will write the unit's story there. For now, however, only the following accounts are known. Some of the material overlaps chronology of the account in the main text. I intentionally kept this out of that section, as there is so little material about the Pacific that both chronicles are better served if the Pacific is discussed on its own.)

THE WAR IN THE Pacific was different than the war in Europe. For one, the war in the Pacific encompassed an area so large and diverse that the Allied command had to be divided into three separate combat zones: the South Pacific theater, commanded by Admiral Chester W. Nimitz; the Southwest Pacific theater, commanded by General Douglas MacArthur; and the China, Burma, and India (CBI), or Southeast Asia, theater, commanded by Admiral Lord Louis Mountbatten.

But, more critical, the war in the Pacific was different

in its ideology. The Japanese lived and fought by the Bushido code, which taught that surrender was a dishonorable act. Prisoners of war, consequently, deserved to live only in disgrace and hardship. POWs were to be treated as slaves—starved, beaten, and put to labor for long hours.

Mistreatment of POWs was further supported by the fact that, whereas Japan had signed the Geneva Convention sanctions on warfare, their legislative Diet had not ratified the signing at the time war was declared. They were not bound to the treaty, and their long-standing cultural codes could prevail.

While rumors of POW mistreatment filtered back to the United States, it was not until late 1942 that confirmation of abuses reached Washington. Soldiers and sailors who had evaded surrender in the Philippines sailed in open boats across the eighteen hundred miles of ocean to Australia, bringing with them personal accounts of beatings, starvation, disease, and multiple executions. Soon confirmation of these reports began to arrive from England, where British troops who had escaped from Hong Kong and the Dutch East Indies were filing similar firsthand accounts of Japanese cruelty.

In repeated protests, Secretary of State Cordell Hull sent official notes to Japan's warlords advising them that they would be held accountable for their mistreatment of Allied prisoners. Japan ignored these communications.

Meanwhile, Red Cross food and medical parcels, carried aboard the Swedish liner *Gripsholm,* continued arriving in Japan, but the supplies were not issued to the POWs.

Washington, recognizing that diplomatic channels were proving unsuccessful, turned to the military for assistance. But the Prisoner of War Branch of the Military Intelligence Service was still a fledgling agency. Colonel J. Edward Johnston and Major Robley Winfrey were rushing to get MIS-X into service and were at a loss to recommend any action that could alleviate conditions in the Orient. The basis for MIS-X operations in Europe would not prove successful in the East: MIS-X had no code users in the Pacific theater even if mail could get through, and because POWs would stand out as Caucasians in a world of Asians, MIS-X E&E procedures were useless. As the following accounts indicate, whatever would happen in the Pacific theater with regard to POW E&E activity would result as much from individual initiative as from coordinated, centralized policy.

E&E IN SOUTHEAST ASIA

Early in the war, MI-9 had a man in the Hong Kong area, Lieutenant Colonel Sir Lindsay Ride, who on his own began collecting intelligence and setting up "rat lines" to aid escapers and evaders. Colonel Ride's small unit received official approval from Brigadier G. E. Grimsdale, the British military attaché in Chungking, and soon acquired the name British Army Aid Group (BAAG). British records concerning BAAG are sealed until the year 2010, and so little is known of this unit beyond that it set up its headquarters in Kuei-lin, in the Kwangsi Chuang region of China, and functioned for over three years.

Familiar with and citing Colonel Ride's efforts, however, Bridagier Norman Crockatt of MI-9 urged Colonel J. Edward Johnston to establish an American E&E operation in the Southeast Pacific theater. Upon learning of BAAG's operations, Colonel Catesby ap Jones and Winfrey felt that perhaps MIS-X could successfully extend its activities into the same area, and Johnston was requested to dispatch an officer to that area for an evaluation.

Johnston selected First Lieutenant Barclay P. Schoyer for the mission, and the choice could not have been better made. Schoyer was not only recognized for his courage and capability, but he spoke fluent Mandarin Chinese. In early 1943 he winged his way across the Pacific to gather information, much as Winfrey had sailed across the Atlantic to compile information about MI-9's work in Europe.

Arriving in Kuei-lin, Schoyer lost little time in contacting Colonel Ride at BAAG headquarters. Under Ride's guidance, Schoyer learned of the potential for an American unit in the area and traveled through some of the jungle terrain, gaining a firsthand familiarity of the hardships that downed airmen would encounter. He recommended to Colonel Johnston that MIS-X begin operations in Southeast Asia. Johnston, after receiving approval from the Pentagon and State Department to set up a unit, selected Colonel A. R. Wichtrich to command the newly established Air Ground Aid Service (AGAS) in the region.

Colonel Wichtrich chose K'un-ming as his unit's headquarters, as this enabled him to set up accessible outposts at various points in the jungle along the routes flown by the U.S. Air Transport Command (ATC) and the Twentieth Air Force, which flew missions between Calcutta and K'un-ming. K'un-ming was also central enough that he could set up accessible outposts for escapers and evaders coming northwest from the huge POW colony at Hong Kong.

Like the fictional outposts depicted in the musical *South Pacific,* the real outposts in Southeast Asia were dangerous and lonely. A single officer with a radio operator lived in a remote area, listening twenty-four hours a day for a "Mayday" or an alert from Wichtrich advising them that an airplane was down. If the downed plane's coordinates were in their area, the two men would set out to locate the craft and, if its personnel were ambulatory, lead the crew back to the outpost until help arrived for the survivors. If a crewman could not be moved, the two men would radio a call, and a small L-1 plane would land in a nearby clearing and evacuate the man.

MIS-X personnel working full time in AGAS were not familiar with the operation of MIS-X at Fort Hunt. They were few in number—Major Leo Crosson thinks only twelve officers and enlisted men—and were assisted by servicemen obtained from units stationed in Southeast Asia who were assigned to MIS-X on temporary duty.

An isolated document on the activities of AGAS discovered in the National Archives is intriguing in that it reveals how hastily temporary personnel were recruited into MIS-X service. The document states that Lieutenant William F. Diebold, of the Air Transport Command, reported for temporary duty on the forenoon of September 9, 1944. At 1600 hours that same afternoon, Lieutenant Diebold parachuted into the Burma jungle to rescue a P-51 pilot who had just been located after wandering in the area for thirty days. Unfortunately, the document does not give details of the rescue, stating that these will be forthcoming in a future report.

MIS-X IN THE SOUTHWEST PACIFIC AREA (SWPA)

Second Lieutenant Harry Osterweis was one of the first five officers selected for MIS-X, as was Second Lieutenant Creighton Churchill. Osterweis soon shipped out to the Southwest Pacific Area:

> Churchill and I didn't even know what unit we were in when we were selected. We were in uniform, and the country was at war—that's all that mattered to us. While we waited for orders to be cut, we wandered around Washington, taking in

the sights. During the evenings, we attended dances in the big hotels. It was great duty.

Then one morning I received orders for movement to London, leaving Churchill—who was assigned to MIS-X at 1142. Upon my arrival in London, I reported to British Intelligence HQ and was directed to MI-9 section, where I spent two months learning to be a briefer to airmen. I was told about contraband in parcels and was taught the secret letter code. But escape and evasion briefing at that time was quite scanty.

Operation TORCH was just beginning in North Africa at the time, and I was shipped there to brief British and American air crews at the new airfields that were being constructed. After a few months, I was just getting settled in when new orders arrived, sending me to Australia.

At Brisbane, I reported to Major Paul S. Kraus, MIS-X station chief in SWPA. Kraus briefed me on the overall picture for the area. Our unit was no longer to be identified as MIS-X; instead, we became a section in a department of the Allied Intelligence Bureau (AIB). AIB was composed of Australian, New Zealand, American, Dutch, and Philippine intelligence services, and included native operatives from New Guinea, the Solomons, Borneo, and a few other islands. It was commanded by Major General Charles Willoughby.

Major Kraus told Osterweis that E&E briefings on Australia were being carried out by MIS-X and MI-9 personnel. Osterweis's primary mission in the Southwest Pacific Area would be to rescue downed Allied airmen in the New Guinea islands, where Osterweis would be stationed at an outpost with a radio operator. Whether the pilot went down over land or water, Osterweis was to handle the rescue from his assigned post.

If the pilot went into the ocean, Osterweis, weather permitting, was to request that the Air Sea Rescue dispatch a Dumbo amphibian to fly to the area. If the water was too choppy for a landing, Osterweis was to appeal to the navy for a small boat.

In the jungle Osterweis would hire natives to guide him to the crewmen and back. Sometimes, the coast watchers, under the command of Lieutenant Commander Eric Feldt of the Royal Australian Navy, would have already picked up the pilot. When Osterweis arrived, the crewman would be drinking gin with his host.

Osterweis recalled one example of how the Japanese used decoys to try to capture the rescuers:

> We had a couple of planes down on the north coast near the village of Aitape. An army recon plane spotted an SOS spelled out on the beach. It looked like a parachute had been cut up to form the signal. It was such a stupid thing to do, as the Japanese could see it as well as we could.
>
> I was assigned to investigate and make the rescue in case it was some of our fellows. But I was suspicious, and requested the army to fly me out in a little recon plane for a closer look. We flew over the area at about one thousand feet, but no one could be seen moving around, and an injured airman could not have laid out that signal. We also knew it had not been there the day before, or our daily reconnaisance patrols would have spotted it.
>
> So, when I landed, I called the army for a loan of a fast, small, armed boat with a half dozen men. They provided me with six eager soldiers and a forty-foot launch with a twenty-millimeter machine gun mounted up forward.

We knew that, if this was a trap, the Japanese would expect us to come straight in from the sea side, because the beach was in a recessed bay formed by a thousand-foot-high rise on all sides. So we approached from the south in the launch and were shielded by the cliff until we were only a thousand feet away from our target. Then we saw Japanese milling about a camouflaged bunker. The boys were ready on the bow and demolished the bunker with twenty-millimeter shells—leaving a few bodies lying on the beach.

Perhaps the most astonishing evasion story in the MIS-X files involves Captain Frederick G. Hargesheimer of the Eighth Photo Squadron, who was shot down over the island of New Britain on June 5, 1943, in a plane vulnerable to attack because the guns had been replaced by cameras:

Blood was streaming down my neck onto the Mae West, and I realized I was hit somewhere on my head. I knew I had to abandon the ship, which was banked in a shallow turn to the right. Pulling on my emergency release, I found that the top hatch didn't completely disengage. Rising up in the seat in an attempt to break it loose, I was sucked out of the cockpit, but managed to get my chute open.

The path of my descent seemed to be leading directly to the spot where my plane had crashed and was now in flames. Pulling on the shrouds, I was able to maneuver away from the fire, and dropped through the trees—pulling my chute down with me. The enemy fighter made a strafing pass, but I was able to hide the chute at the base of a tree and none of the shots hit me.

I opened my jungle emergency evasion pack

[provided by MIS-X] and secured some sulfanilamide for my head wound, and then fashioned on a field dressing. After burying my Mae West and destroying other possible evidence of my presence, I fashioned a carrying pack from the parachute harness and set off to get away from the crash site and possible enemy detection.

The book *Advice to Aircrews for Survival and Evasion* said not to travel too far the first day, so I pitched camp about a mile away from the crash. The book was very helpful in showing me how to construct a tent with my parachute and to use my small rubber boat as a ground sheet.

A heavy rain then stopped my plans to build a fire, and I had the first in a series of sleepless nights.

I nibbled a bit of chocolate, folded my maps and everything into a pack, and guided by the compass from the survival kit, set out for the south coast of New Britain, where I felt my chances for survival were better. Heavy rains continued to make it impossible to have a fire, so I saved my matches in the waterproof container.

After three days, I gave up the idea of following a compass course and followed a small stream which eventually flowed into a larger river. As the water was deep enough, I launched my little rubber boat and paddled my way for several hours. The paddles were not oars, but something like mittens. The sudden appearance of crocodiles off my port bow caused me to abandon the water, and I continued on foot along the bank. Finding a good trail leading downstream, I followed that for four days.

Strangely enough, the small supply of ration "D" chocolate was sufficient to satisfy my hunger during the entire first ten days.

I came upon a small shelter at the bank of the river and decided to set up a more permanent camp. Unfortunately, I had lost my jungle knife and had difficulty securing firewood. Using my last match, I managed to get a fire going but knew it would require constant attention. So I chose to remain at this spot, hoping some natives would return to fish in the river.

Searching about the hut, I discovered some small snail (guama) shells in the old fire bed and deduced they must have been edible. So I searched the river and in the rapids found an abundance of "guams." When roasted in the fire for several minutes, a portion of the guam detaches itself from the shell and it's a simple matter to extract the meat with a sharp, pointed stick.

They tasted quite good. The only other foods I ate were a few red citrus berries and three Java beans. I made several attempts to shoot birds with my pistol, but failed.

I managed to catch a large grasshopper, and securing the line and hood from the survival kit, I set it in the river that night. Returning the next morning, I found the whole works carried away. Minutes later, I saw a big fish swimming in the shallows. In a fit of unrestrained anger, I drew my pistol and fired at him. When the splashes died and the water cleared, I saw him lying on his side. The shot had missed him, but he was stunned. I scrambled into the water, fully dressed, and grabbed dinner.

But food was really secondary, compared to keeping my fire going.

Waking in the night, I once found just a faint glowing, and only with luck was I able to fan a flame onto some dry grass I kept handy. Once, when searching for other food to supplement my diet of snails, my sixth sense told me to return to camp without delay. I approached the camp at top speed, out of breath and peering intently for a glimpse of smoke. But only a pile of dead ashes greeted me. Fire was my only hope to continue living—not only to cook with, but to keep out the crawling intruders at night. I began an earnest prayer as I dropped to my knees and started blowing in the ashes until a faint wisp of smoke appeared. Again, the Lord had placed His hand on my shoulder, as the dried grass I held in my hand ignited.

A month had now passed, and it's hard to put into words what gave me the strength to keep going. But it is my honest conclusion that I developed the patience to accept my situation with the feeling that I was not alone and I would eventually be saved.

The sixth of July was very much like all other days I had endured on the island. After a morning swim, it was a hike through the jungle to gather my firewood, then an afternoon nap. There was a noticeable absence of mosquitoes during the day, so I saved the quinine for nighttime only. I also limited myself to one half-tablet of salt per day. So far, the survival and evasion kit had served me well, and I had warm feelings for the people who had conceived and packed it, realizing how they had anticipated my every essential need.

Late one afternoon, while gathering snails for the evening meal, I was startled by the appearance of a native canoe being pushed around the bend of the river by a group of natives. They saw me about the same time. There was some jabbering and pointing in my direction, and one young man rushed up to me waving a notebook and shouting, "You number one, Master! Number one!" I was so overjoyed to see another human after thirty-four days of solitary life that it was difficult for me to control myself.

Upon investigating the notebook, I learned that these natives had provided food and care for an Australian and three American airmen. This was conclusive evidence of the loyalty of the natives, and I had no hesitancy in placing myself in their charge. My first task was to win their friendship, so I gave them some tobacco strips from the survival kit and the coins I had in my pocket.

The dominant young male native had worked for Europeans on New Britain and seemed to understand simple English words much better than my timid attempts at pidgin. I gathered that his name was Luluai.

That evening, we sat around a glowing fire as I was introduced to taro to go with the fish they had no trouble catching in the river.

Luluai assured me that there were no Japanese at his village on the beach and that it would be quite safe for me. He said it was also a good spot for signaling friendly aircraft. I learned later that this party of natives had journeyed upriver for the specific purpose of locating American or Australian airmen.

During the trip downriver the next morning, they took special pains to hide the canoe along the shore whenever the sounds of planes were heard. Upon approaching the mouth of the river, we picked up another canoe load of natives who went on ahead to ensure that the beach was free of hostile "Kanaka" (Japanese). After the "All clear" was called out to us, we proceeded to the mouth of the river, where a group of small huts stood on the edge of the lagoon.

All of the relatives came by to shake hands and pay their respects. A feast was prepared and after filling myself on wild pig and native vegetables, I stretched out on my bed in Luluai's hut and began making up for lost sleep.

In the morning, Luluai decided it would be best not to spread word of my arrival and that I should remain here at the mouth of the river instead of proceeding to their main village several miles down the beach. As I placed myself in their charge, I did as he suggested. Two days later, two Methodist mission boys brought me an English Bible to read.

My stay at this village was frequently interrupted by the appearance of hostile native canoes, and I was obliged to seek cover in the bush. Then one day while I was hiding out, I had an attack of malaria fever. Unfortunately, I did not realize I had the fever and failed to use the few quinine tablets I had left. As a result, I became very ill. During this period of illness, I lived for more than a week on breast milk from Luluai's wife. Then, a police boy, passing through, advised me that a German Catholic padre and four brothers were living in the bush not too far away.

I sent the boy with a note to the padre, asking for medical help. I wrote the paragraph in German, since I had taken the language in school. The next day, in answer to my appeal, the padre sent the police boy back with some Dr. Morris' Root Pills, which, according to the direction on the bottle, were a "sure cure" for all ills and ailments. Miraculously I began to improve soon after I started taking the pills.

My thanks to Dr. Morris, the padre, but most of all to Luluai's wife.

A short time later, after I had recovered from the fever, the natives felt it would be healthier for me if I lived nearer the beach. So I was moved to a hut that was built for me and stayed until the third of November. On that day, a native boy who had previously been evacuated from his village with the Australian and American airmen returned with a note asking I join another white party some miles away. I was not yet strong enough to make such a journey and sent a note telling of my condition, giving my name, rank, and organization.

Several days later, a member of the white party appeared at the village, bringing welcome medical supplies. He told me he was an E&E intelligence officer [this was an MIS-X officer] and that he would keep in close touch with me, but he had to return to his duties. I asked him to send a signal to the Fifth Air Force requesting that I be placed on detached service and allowed to remain on New Britain as a radio operator.

Two weeks later, the white man returned with a portable radio transmitter and advised me that my request to become part of the E&E team had been granted.

Captain Fred Hargesheimer had experienced the helpless, lonely feelings of a downed aviator and believed that remaining on the island conducting E&E work would make a greater contribution to the war effort than flying photo recon missions. He was made a member of the MIS-X team in the Southwest Pacific.

On February 4, 1944, Captain Hargesheimer and an Australian coast watcher were ordered off the island for security reasons. The nearby submarine USS *Gato* then received the following orders: "MISSION: To remove from Manatanakunai, Open Bay, New Britain, one Australian coast watcher, a Capt. Hargesheimer, and as many shot-down Allied airmen as may be gathered there."

At 2010 hours, on February 5, the coast watcher and four aviators were picked up in two rubber boats and began to row back to the submarine. "Having covered about two hundred yards of the return journey," the coast watcher reported, "we heard a commotion on the beach. Then a blinker light began signaling. It read: 'Sixty-seven more aviators here.'"

Captain Fred Hargesheimer had paid back his debt.

THE FINAL STORY OF THE PACIFIC THEATER

"Hideki Tojo, the 'Razor,' who sent millions of many nations to their deaths while he was Japan's premier, botched his own suicide today," read the opening lines of the lead story in the *New York Times* on September 12, 1945. The article then went on to relate that George E. Jones, correspondent for the *Times,* was accompanying two American army officers sent to arrest General Tojo at his Tokyo home. Upon entering Tojo's residence, the three men found him locked in his bedroom, refusing to come out.

Suddenly a shot came from the room and Jones and the two officers broke down the door and found Tojo standing unsteadily on his feet, holding a smoking pistol in his hand. Using a .32-caliber Colt automatic pistol, Tojo had shot himself in the chest rather than face an Allied military tribunal for war crimes. A doctor was quickly summoned, and Tojo was given a transfusion.

He lived to be convicted of war crimes and hanged as payment for his inhumanities.

What the article was unable to report was that the arresting team that went to Tojo's residence that day was commanded by Major Paul S. Kraus—MIS-X station chief in Australia.

POSTSCRIPT TO WINFREY IN THE PACIFIC

(Author's note: The following information about Colonel Robley Winfrey's activities in the Pacific theater was learned years after MIS-X had been dismantled. It is added here rather than in the body of the book, as I tried to reveal there only what was known within MIS-X at the time.)

IN EARLY 1944 MIS-X learned that Japan was allowing coolie vendors into the POW camps to sell fruits and vegetables. Winfrey knew that Colonel A. R. Wichtrich, MIS-X chief in China, had thought up the idea of using false bottoms in the coolie baskets to smuggle supplies in to the POWs. With his meager budget, Wichtrich was buying fruits and vegetables and paying the vendors to carry the food into the camps. In return for the payment, the vendors carried money, quinine, and vitamins in their baskets. It was a system that was working, but it lacked the desired volume.

Winfrey had a simple plan in mind and shared his thoughts with Colonel Johnston. "Would Chiang Kai-shek permit two million dollars worth of his nation's currency to be printed in the United States if the money was backed by the American dollar?" he asked.

Johnston found the idea intriguing, and using military channels, he requested the aid of Assistant Secretary of State Dean Acheson in obtaining the necessary approvals. Acheson was able to accomplish this, and this was the money that arrived in banded boxes at 1142 shortly before Winfrey left the United States.

When Winfrey left 1142, he flew to Pearl Harbor, where he visited with Admiral Nimitz and briefed the admiral on the MIS-X mission. Receiving the admiral's permission to work in the Southwest Pacific Area, Winfrey then flew on to Agana, Guam, where the money had been forwarded. Winfrey then took the two million dollars in Chinese yuan and made his way to K'un-ming, China, arriving in early October 1944. He reported to Colonel Wichtrich and handed the money over to him for use in the Asian camps.

Winfrey remained under Wichtrich's command until the end of the war, prowling the Southwest Pacific theater, helping to enlarge the coolie net, and assisting in E&E activities throughout the area.

APPENDIX II

—✕——✕—

Secret Letter Codes

An early British code reveals how a message can be hidden within a seemingly innocuous letter. The decoded solution and grid reveal the message. For purposes of illustration, the key words have been highlighted in the text of the letter here.

SAMPLE LETTER

3/7/42

Dear Ellen,

How good to hear from you again.

Just returned from the STATION where we unloaded a supply TRAIN all morning. I damn NEAR sprained my back lugging all THE crates of food to CAMP. There's a sergeant here named NORTH who lives just outside OF Salinas! Small world. His uncle MILES works in the sausage FACTORY where Aunt Clarice worked. For TWO years I've been craving GROUND sausage or almost any meat UNDER the sun. Given nothing but powdered eggs and turnips; it's a wonder we've survived this long.

Can you send me books to read, like novels and maybe biographies; sure would appreciate it. Healthwise I'm fine, just bored and waiting for this to end.

Love you always,
Bill.

TO DECODE LETTER

In the sample letter, a date written out as "March 7, 1942" would tell the reader there is no code in the letter. But a date line using all numerals, such as "3/7/42," indicates a code is present.

To determine the number of words in the message, multiply the number of letters in the first two words of the first line. For example, in the sample, "How good" is 3 times 4 letters, for a total of 12 words.

A grid block is drawn with three squares across and four squares down. The code words are entered into the grid block beginning at the top left square, proceeding to the right until all squares are filled in.

The code word frequency in the sample is 5/6, meaning that beginning with the second line, first the fifth word, STATION, and then the sixth word, TRAIN, are entered into the grid. Continuing, the fifth word, NEAR, and the sixth word, THE, are entered on the grid; the words are counted and entered until all blocks are filled.

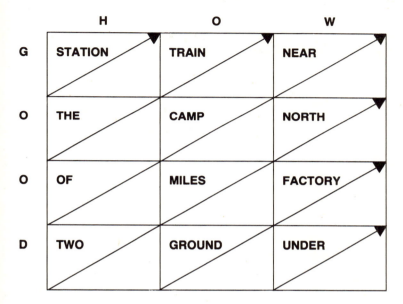

The grid is read in the direction of the arrows, begin-
ning with the bottom right box. The message reads: UN-
DER GROUND FACTORY TWO MILES NORTH OF
CAMP NEAR THE TRAIN STATION.

APPENDIX III

—— ✕ —————— ✕ ——

German POW Camp Locations

Stalagen
(main camps, usually for enlisted men)

2A	Neubrandenburg
2B	Hammerstein (99 work camps near Köslin and Stolp)
2E	Schwerin
3A	Luckenwalde
3B	Fürstenburg (plus work camps 1-5)
3C	Alt Drewitz
3D	Steglitz
4A	Hohnstein (13 work camps near Dresden)
4B	Mühlberg
4C	Wistritz
4D	Torgau
4D/2	Annaburg
4F	Hartmannsdorf

4G	Oschatz
5A	Ludwigsburg
5B	Villingen
5C	Offenburg
6C	Osnabrück
6G	Bonn
6J	Krefeld
7A	Moosburg
7B	Memmingen
8A	Görlitz
8B	Teschen
8C	Sagan
9B	Bad Orb
9C	Bad Sulza
10B	Bremervörde
10C	Nienburg
11A	Altengrabow
11B	Fallingbostel
12A	Limburg
12D	Waldbreitbach
12F	Freinsheim
13B	Weiden
13C	Hammelburg
13D	Nürnberg
17A	Kaisersteinbrück
17B	Krems
18A	Wolfsberg
18C	Markt Pongau
20A	Toruń (Thorn)
20B	Marienburg
21A	Posen (Poznań)
344	Lamsdorf
357	Orske
383	Hohenfels
398	Pupping
Work Camp 21	Blechhammer

Marlagen/Milagen and Oflagen
(sailor/military camps and camps for officers)

Marlag/Milag	Tarmstedt
4C	Colditz
7B	Eichstätt
9A/H	Spangenberg
9A/Z	Rotenburg
10B	Nienburg
11(79)	Braunschweig
13B	Hammelburg
21B(64)	Schubin

Stalag Luft Camps
(camps for airmen)

1	Barth
3	Sagan
4	Grosstychow
6	Heydekrug
7	Bankau

Dulag Luft Camps
(transit camps for airmen)

Wetzlar

Hospitals

4A	Hohnstein
4G	Leipzig
5B	Rottenmunster
6C	Lingen
6G	Gerresheim

6J	Düsseldorf
8A	Freising
8C	Ebelsbach
9B	Bad Soden
9C(a)	Obermassfeld
9C(b)	Meiningen
9C(c)	Hildburghausen
10A	Schleswig
10B	Sandbostel
13D	Nürnberg
18A/Z	Spittal
Marine	Cuxhaven
Airmen	Wismar

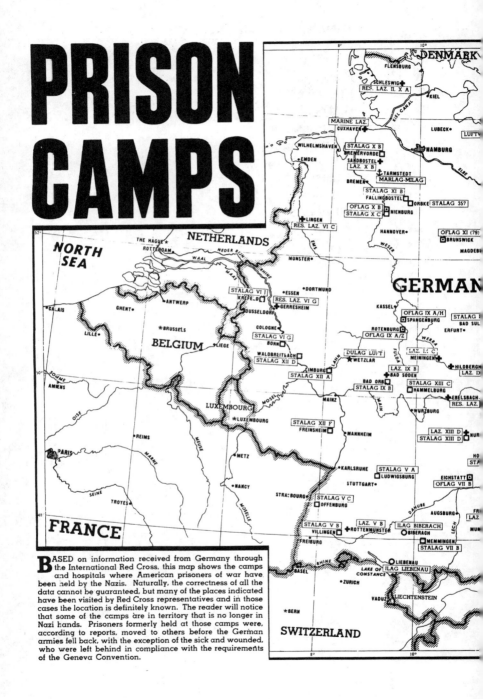

PRISON CAMPS

BASED on information received from Germany through the International Red Cross, this map shows the camps and hospitals where American prisoners of war have been held by the Nazis. Naturally, the correctness of all the data cannot be guaranteed, but many of the places indicated have been visited by Red Cross representatives and in those cases the location is definitely known. The reader will notice that some of the camps are in territory that is no longer in Nazi hands. Prisoners formerly held at those camps were, according to reports, moved to others before the German armies fell back, with the exception of the sick and wounded, who were left behind in compliance with the requirements of the Geneva Convention.

NOTES

IN CITING WORKS IN the notes, short titles have generally been used. Title categories of National Archive material cite only the Record Group here; complete titles may be found in the Bibliography. Public depositories frequently cited have been identified with the following abbreviations:

USAFHRC   United States Air Force
           Historical Research Center,
           Maxwell Air Force Base,
           Montgomery, Alabama
WNRC   Washington National Records
           Center, Suitland, Maryland

CHAPTER 1

1. Untitled document charging the training group with making provisions for army escape and evasion activities, RG 319, WNRC.

2. History of the Military Intelligence Division, chap. 5, 170.22, USAFHRC.
3. Special Use Permit Authorizing Use of Land in Fort Hunt, RG 319, WNRC.
4. Chris Ulrich, "Fort Hunt as WW II POW Camp Captures Alexandria's Interest," *Alexandria Gazette,* 22 August 1985.

CHAPTER 2

1. Establishment of a Unit to Deal with Prisoner of War Escape Methods, RG 332, WNRC.
2. Robley E. Winfrey, interview with author, Arlington, VA, 4 March 1987.
3. Ibid.
4. Establishment of a Unit to Deal with Prisoner of War Escape Methods, RG 332, WNRC.
5. Ibid.
6. Ibid.
7. M. R. D. Foot and J. M. Langley, MI-9: Escape and Evasion 1939–1945 (Boston: Little, Brown, 1979), 47.
8. Winfrey interview, 4 March 1987.

CHAPTER 3

1. Harry L. Osterweis, interview with author, New York, NY, 3 October 1987; letter to author, 2 February 1988.
2. Memorandum For: Chief Army Security Agency, Subject: MIS-X Codes, RG 319, WNRC.
3. Frederick W. Siegel, telephone interview with author, 4 January 1987.

CHAPTER 4

1. Winfrey interview, 4 March 1987.
2. War Department, MIS, Report 621, 142.761, USAFHRC.
3. Albert P. Clark, Jr., interview with author, Colorado Springs, CO, 12 August 1986.

CHAPTER 5

1. Messages Received to Date, RG 319, WNRC.
2. Ibid.
3. John Bowman, telephone interview with author, 1 June 1987.
4. Horace Dale Bowman, telephone interview with author, 4 June 1987; letter to author, 30 June 1987.

CHAPTER 6

1. War Department, MIS, Report 647, 142.761, USAFHRC.
2. War Department, MIS, Report 645, 142.761, USAFHRC.
3. John K. Waters, interview with author, Potomac, MD, 28 February 1987.
4. This message was sent to all camps receiving contraband articles in parcels that were shipped by MIS-X. For examples of messages that were sent and received by POWs, see: War Department, MIS, Report 437, 142.761, USAFHRC.

CHAPTER 7

1. Messages Received to Date, RG 319, WNRC.
2. Ibid.
3. Ibid.
4. Ibid.

CHAPTER 8

1. Operations History of 6801 MIS-X Detachment, RG 332, WNRC.
2. Repatriation Report #2, Repatriation from Germany, RG 332, WNRC; Memorandum for Major John H. Star, 142.765, USAFHRC; Notes Taken by Technical Section, MIS-X, POW Branch, 142.765, USAFHRC.
3. Ibid.
4. Anecdotes on Evasion and Escape for the Use of Intelligence Officers, RG 319, WNRC.

CHAPTER 9

1. Kenneth Kurtenbach, telephone interview with author, 12 December 1988; Western Europe, E&E Report 434, 142.7621, USAFHRC.

CHAPTER 11

1. Claude Murray, "Camp History of Stalag Luft III", Part 3 (Air Force Escape and Evasion Society, n.d.), 12.
2. Ibid., 13.
3. Ibid., 14–18; Arthur A. Durand, "Stalag Luft III," (Ph.D. diss., Louisiana State University, 1976), 404–6.
4. David M. Jones, telephone interview with author, 13 September 1986.

CHAPTER 12

1. Winfrey interview, 4 March 1987.
2. Clayton Hutton, *Official Secret* (New York: Crown, 1961), 23.
3. R. T. Goldsmith, telephone interview with author, 28 March 1986.
4. Jack Oliver, interview with author, Grand Junction, CO, 13 August 1986.
5. Ray F. Ostrander, telephone interview with author, 16 February 1989.

CHAPTER 13

1. American Prisoners of War in Germany, 142.7041-2, USAFHRC.
2. War Department, MIS, Report 618, 142.761, USAFHRC.
3. Ibid.
4. Memorandum from HQ ETO, AC of S, G-2, to AC of S, G-2, SHEAF, subject, Proposal by Prisoners for Rescue from German Prison Camps, RG 332, WNRC.
5. Ibid.

6. Pentagon meetings detailing rescue plans were related to author by Winfrey at the time they took place.

CHAPTER 14

1. Comité international de la croix-rouge, Geneva, to War Organization of the British Red Cross Society and Order of St. John of Jerusalem, RG 319, WNRC.
2. British Red Cross Society to Leslie Winterbottom, RG 319, WNRC.

CHAPTER 15

1. MID, G-2, Memorandum, Proposed Message to US Prisoners of War on Escaping, RG 319, WNRC.
2. W. James Billig, telephone interview with author, 13 September 1986.
3. John M. Bennett, interview with author, Colorado Springs, CO, 12 August 1986.
4. Ibid.
5. Alvin W. Vogtle, telephone interview with author, 1 December 1986.
6. Ibid.
7. Albert P. Clark, Jr., "Intelligence Potential of Prisoners of War" (Clark Collection, U.S. Air Force Academy Library, 1947), 21.
8. Joe Bell, letter to author, 6 November 1986.
9. War Department, Repatriation Reports, Report 26, 142.765, USAFHRC.
10. Ibid.

CHAPTER 16

1. War Department, Repatriation Reports, Report 28, 142.765, USAFHRC.

CHAPTER 17

1. Untitled document lists categories pertaining to "Red Cross parcels," "POW mail," "Escape expedients obtained or manufactured in captivity," "Underground contacts," and "German preventive measures"; sources listed are German, probably from captured enemy documents, and list "Countermeasures" to be taken by German camp security staffs; RG 319, WNRC.
2. Reinhold Eggers, *Colditz: The German Side of the Story* (New York: W. W. Norton, 1961), 119–20.
3. War Department, MIS, Escape & Evasion Bulletin #7—MIS-X, 170.2258-16, USAFHRC.
4. Ibid.

CHAPTER 18

1. War Department, MIS, Report 435, 142.761, USAFHRC.
2. Ibid.
3. War Department, MIS, Report 437, 142.761, USAFHRC.
4. War Department, MIS, Report 435, 142.761, USAFHRC.
5. War Department, MIS, Report 437, 142.761, USAFHRC.

CHAPTER 19

1. War Department, MIS, Report 661, 142.761, USAFHRC; letter, Kenneth Kurtenbach to Andrew Hasselbring, 28 August 1987.
2. Kenneth Kurtenbach, telephone interview with author, 15 March 1987.
3. War Department, MIS, Report 651, 142.761, USAFHRC.
4. War Department, MIS, Report 661, 142.761, USAFHRC; letter, Kurtenbach to Hasselbring, 28 August 1987.
5. Kurtenbach interview, 15 March 1987.
6. Ibid.
7. John L. Susan, letter to author, 20 December 1987.
8. Kurtenbach interview, 15 March 1987.

CHAPTER 20

1. Eggers, 23.
2. W. T. "Lulu" Lawton, letters to author, 5 March 1987, 2 June 1987.
3. Eggers, 118.

CHAPTER 21

1. Arthur A. Durand, "Stalag Luft III," 186–87.
2. Delmar T. Spivey, *POW Odyssey* (Attleboro, MA: Colonial Lithograph, 1984), 187.
3. War Department, MIS, Report 646, 142.761, USAFHRC.
4. Spivey, 105–7.
5. James Billig, telephone interview with author, 13 September 1986.
6. War Department, MIS, Report 620, 142.761, USAFHRC.
7. Jones, interview, 13 September 1986.
8. Durand, 384–85.
9. Spivey, 135.
10. Ibid., 154.
11. Ibid., 175.

CHAPTER 22

1. Memorandum for Colonel J. E. Johnston, Camps in Germany Holding American Ps/w Enveloped by Russian Advance, RG 319, WNRC.

ACKNOWLEDGMENTS

GRATEFUL ACKNOWLEDGMENT is made to the following for their generous assistance in making this book possible:

Dr. George Chalou, U.S. National Archives

Mr. Richard Boylan, U.S. National Archives

Mr. George Kitchens, Air Library, Maxwell Air Force Base

Captain Lucinda M. Hackman, Air Intelligence Library, Bolling Field Air Force Base, Maryland

General John K. Waters, Commander in Chief, U.S. Army, Pacific (ret.); POW, CU, Oflag 64

Lieutenant General Albert P. Clark, Jr., U.S. Air Force (ret.); "Big X," Stalag Luft III

Mrs. Delmar T. Spivey, widow of Major General Delmar T. Spivey, Senior Allied Officer, Center Compound, Stalag Luft III

Major General David M. "Tokyo" Jones, U.S. Air Force (ret.); Tunnelman, Stalag Luft III

Colonel John M. Bennett, U.S. Air Force (ret.); Property Master, Stalag Luft III

Mr. Duane Reed, Archivist, Special Collections, U.S. Air Force Academy Library

Mr. Silvio A. Bedini, Deputy Director, Smithsonian Institution; MIS-X cryptoanalyst

Colonel Robley E. Winfrey, Commanding Officer, Technical Section, MIS-X

Major Leo H. Crosson, Commanding Officer, Technical Section, MIS-X

Mr. Carl Peterson, Warehouse personnel, MIS-X

Mr. John Slack, Adjutant, Oflag 64

Mr. Kenneth J. Kurtenbach, Man of Confidence, Stalag 17-B

Mr. Françoise Perret, Comité International de la Croix-Rouge (International Red Cross)

Mr. Harry Baughn, POW, Camp Timisul de Jos, Romania

Mrs. Claudia Bennett Layton, radiologist, Salem, Oregon

Mr. Joe Bell, parcelman, Stalag Luft III

Mr. James Billig, POW, CU, Stalag Luft III

Mrs. Barbara Bond, British Embassy, Washington, D.C.

Mr. William R. Cory, POW, Oflag 64

Mr. Mark Curtis, POW, Stalag 17-B

Mr. Gotfried Dietze, German censor, Oflag 64

Mr. Jerry Flemmons, *Dallas–Fort Worth Star-Telegram*

Mrs. Betty Gallegos, POWs of America, Oregon chapter

Mr. Charles Conway, Gillette Razor Company

Dr. James Gilbert, Army Intelligence Command

Mr. John Finnigan, Army Intelligence Command

Mrs. Margery Griffith, U.S. Playing Card Company

Mr. Fred Hargesheimer, South Pacific pilot

Mr. Thomas Harvey, United Press International

Mr. Richard Seaman, Imperial War Museum, London

RAF Museum, Hendon, England

Mr. Richard W. Kimball, author, *Clipped Wings*

Dr. Brooks Kleber, Deputy Chief Historian, U.S. Army History Center

Mr. Keith Melton, U.S. Intelligence Officer

Mr. Jack Oliver, POW, Stalag Luft III

Lieutenant Colonel Harry Osterweis, MIS-X, South Pacific

Mr. David Pollak, parcelman, Stalag Luft III

Dr. Walter Pforzheimer, U.S. Intelligence Officer

Ms. Elizabeth Hooks, American Red Cross, Washington, D.C.

Colonel Jerry Sage, POW, Stalag Luft III, author, *Sage*

Colonel Fredrick W. Siegel, chief U.S. censor, World War II

Mrs. Edward O. Thomas, daughter of Colonel J. Edward Johnston, MIS-X

Colonel John Van Vliet, U.S. Army (ret.); Oflag 64 CU

Mr. Alvin "Sammy" Vogtle, Stalag Luft III

Mr. Charles Worman, archivist, Air Force Museum, Dayton, Ohio

Mr. Francis Paules, Man of Confidence, CU, Stalag Luft I, IV, VI

Mr. Charles Holtzman

Lieutenant Colonel C. A. Williamson, Thirty-sixth Division Historian, Oflag 64

Mr. Ray F. Ostrander, vice-president, U.S. Playing Card Company

Mr. Charles Smith-Fraser, Devon, England

Professor M. R. D. Foot, author, *MI-9*

Captain William T. Lawton, Colditz

Mr. Victor Watson, John Waddington Company, Leeds, U.K.

David Morgan Literary Agency, Portland, Oregon

Mr. Mark H. Berkowitz, St. Martin's Press

Ms. Linda Venator, who did a terrific job as copy editor

Mr. Steven J. Ovens, my researcher, without whom there would be no book

BIBLIOGRAPHY

UNPUBLISHED MATERIALS

United States Air Force Historical Research Center, Maxwell Air Force Base, Montgomery, Alabama

American Prisoners of War in Germany. 15 July 1944. 142.7041-2.
American Prisoners of War in Germany. 1 November 1945. 142.7041-3.
History of the Military Intelligence Division. December 1941–September 1945. 170.22.
War Department, Repatriation Reports. 142.765.
War Department, Military Intelligence Service. 142.761.

U.S. Air Force Academy Library, Special Collections Room, Colorado Springs, Colorado

Clark, Albert P., Jr. Photographic Work. Clark Collection, 1945.
———. Radio and News Service. Clark Collection, 1945.
———. Intelligence Potential of Prisoners of War. Clark Collection, 1947.
Durand, Arthur A. "Stalag Luft III: An American Experience

in a World War II German Prisoner of War Camp."
Ph.D. diss., Louisiana State University, 1976.

Goodrich, Charles G. "History of the USAAF Prisoners of
War of the South Compound, Stalag Luft III." Photocopy. 1945.

Lindeiner, Friedrich-Wilhelm von. "The Memoirs of Colonel
Friedrich-Wilhelm von Lindeiner-Wildau, Kommandant,
Stalag Luft III." Trans. Berthold Geiss; ed. Arthur A.
Durand. Photocopy. N.d.

Mulligan, Thomas E., Lyman B. Burbank, and Robert R.
Brunn. "History of Center Compound, Stalag Luft III,
Sagan, Germany." Photocopy. 1945.

Murray, Claude. "Camp History of Stalag Luft III (Sagan),
Air Force Personnel, April 1942–January 1945." Air
Force Escape and Evasion Society. Photocopy. N.d

Washington National Records Center, Suitland, Maryland

Records of the Army Staff. Records of the Office of Assistant
Chief of Staff, G-2, Intelligence. Record Group 319.

Records of United States Theaters of War, World War II. European Theater of Operations, MIS. Record Group 332.

Records of the War Department General and Special Staffs.
Records of the Office of the Director of Intelligence
(G-2). Record Group 165.

SELECTED BOOKS

Bailey, Ronald H., ed. *Prisoners of War*. Chicago: Time-Life
Books, 1981.

Barker, A. J. *Prisoners of War*. New York: Universe Books,
1975.

Baybutt, Ron. *Colditz: The Great Escapes*. Boston: Little,
Brown, 1982.

Bowman, Martin. *Home by Christmas*. Northamptonshire,
England: Patrick Stephens, 1987.

Brickhill, Paul. *The Great Escape*. New York: W. W. Norton,
1950.

Collins, Douglas. *P.O.W.* New York: W. W. Norton, 1968.

Crawley, Adrian. *Escape from Germany.* London: Her Majesty's Stationary Office, 1985.

Daniel, Eugene L. *In the Presence of Mine Enemies.* Attleboro, MA: Colonial Lithograph, 1983.

Eggers, Reinhold. *Colditz: The German Side of the Story.* New York: W. W. Norton, 1961.

———. *Colditz Recaptured.* London: Robert Hale, 1973.

Evans, A. J. *The Escaping Club.* London: The Bodley Head, 1921.

Foot, M. R. D. *S.O.E. in France.* London: Her Majesty's Stationary Office, 1976.

———. *Resistance.* New York: McGraw-Hill, 1979.

Foot, M. R. D., and J. M. Langley. *MI-9: Escape and Evasion 1939–1945.* Boston: Little, Brown, 1979.

Foy, David A. *For You the War Is Over.* New York: Stein and Day, 1984.

Fraser-Smith, Charles. *The Secret War of Charles Fraser-Smith.* London: Michael Joseph, 1983.

———. *Secret Warriors.* Exeter, England: The Paternoster Press, 1984.

Garret, Richard. *P.O.W.: The Uncivil Face of War.* Devon, England: David and Charles, 1981.

Graham, Burton. *Escape from the Swastika.* London: Marshall Cavendish, 1975.

Green, J. M. *From Colditz in Code.* London: Robert Hale, 1971.

Hutton, Clayton. *Official Secret.* New York: Crown, 1961.

Kimball, R. W., and O. M. Chiesel. *Clipped Wings.* N.p., n.d.

Langley, J. M. *Fight Another Day.* London: Magnum Press, 1980.

Larvie, E. H. *The Man Who Came in from Colditz.* London: Robert Hale, 1975.

Levie, Howard. *Prisoners of War in International Armed Conflict.* International Law Studies, vol. 59. Newport, RI: Naval War College, 1977.

Montagu, Ewen. *The Man Who Never Was.* New York: Penguin Books, 1956.

Moore, John H. *The Faustball Tunnel.* New York: Random House, 1978.

Neave, Airey. *They Have Their Exits*. London: Hodder and Stoughton, 1953.

———. *Saturday at MI-9*. London: Trinity Press, 1969.

Newby, Leroy W. *Target Ploesti*. Novato, CA: Presidio Press, 1983.

Pape, Richard. *Boldness Be My Friend*. London: Elek Books, 1953.

Reid, P. R. *The Colditz Story*. New York: J. B. Lippincott, 1953.

———. *Men of Colditz*. New York: J. B. Lippincott, 1954.

———. *Colditz: The Full Story*. New York: St. Martin's Press, 1984.

———. *Prisoner of War*. New York: Beaufort, 1984.

Romilly, Giles, and Michael Alexander. *Hostages of Colditz*. New York: Praeger Publishers, 1973.

Sage, Jerry. *Sage: Dagger of the O.S.S.* Wayne, PA: Miles Standish Press, 1985.

Simmons, Kenneth W. *Kriegie*. New York: Thomas Nelson and Sons, 1960.

Spivey, Delmar T. *POW Odyssey*. Attleboro, MA: Colonial Lithograph, 1984.

Toland, John. *The Last 100 Days*. New York: Random House, 1966.

Veterans Administration. *POW: Study of Former Prisoners of War*. Washington, DC: Government Printing Office, 1980.

Williams, Eric. *The Tunnel Escape*. New York: Berkley, 1952.

———. *The Wooden Horse*. New York: Abelard-Schuman, 1958.

INDEX

Korean War, 2
Kraus, Major Paul S., 223, 233
Kroner, Brigadier General H. A., 118
Kuhn, Colonel (Stalag 17-B), 173
Kurtenbach, Technical Sergeant Kenneth, 75–76, 170–178, 214

LaBrosse, Sergeant Ray, 79
Lancashire Penny Fund, 30, 130
Lawton, Captain William T., 180–182
Layton, Claudia Bennett, 215
Lee, Lieutenant Royal, 51, 122
Lewis's Ltd., 30, 130
Lindeiner, Colonel Friedrich-Wilhelm von, 93, 142–143
Lovos, Sergeant Lawrence C., 72
Luftwaffe, 53, 81, 116, 143

MacArthur, General Douglas, 19, 203–204, 218
Mackemer, Lieutenant Carl C., 158
Man of Confidence (MOC), 43, 152, 172, 173, 214
Maps secretly supplied to POWs
by MI-9, 8–9, 119
by MIS-X, 39, 57, 84, 108–112, 119
Marlagen, locations of, 240
Marshall, General George C., 11, 124–125
Massey, Group Captain Martin, 53, 65
Maxwell Air Force Base Air Library, 209
McNichols, Col., 66
McTighe, Lieutenant James H., 84–85, 104, 113, 151, 156, 205
Medhurst, Vice-Marshall Charles, 11
Meidlein, Private First Class George, 83–84
MI-9 (British Intelligence), 7–11,

MI-9 (British Intelligence) (cont.)
13–14, 17, 25, 29–30, 34–35, 58, 63–64, 71, 103–104, 108, 121, 167, 172, 207, 214, 219, 223
MI-9 (Foot), 207, 209, 216–217
Milagen, locations of, 240
Military Intelligence Division, 2
Military Intelligence-9. See MI-9 (British Intelligence)
Military Intelligence Service, 2–3, 116, 219
Military Intelligence Service-X. See MIS-X
Military Intelligence Service-Y. See MIS-Y
Milligan, Lieutenant T. E., 191
MIS-X
briefing of servicemen in escape and evasion, 16–19, 24, 63–70, 161, 204, 223
Colditz Castle and, 180–184
correspondence section of ("the Creamery"), 17–22
creation and staffing of, 10–17
debriefing liberated POWs, 202–203
distribution of E&E materials and, 29–36, 38–41, 113, 119–121, 133–135, 148–150
end of the war in Europe and, 198–203
financing of, 13, 81–82, 90–91
missions of, 12–13
obliteration of, 1–2, 204–206
Oflag 64 and, 36–52, 115–126, 212
Pacific theater and, 203–204, 218–234
researching to write The Escape Factory, 106, 125–126, 207–217
secrecy about, 5–6
Stalag Luft III and, 55–59, 62, 93, 107–108, 131–135, 144–150, 191
Stalag Luft VI and, 150–155
Stalag VII-A, 172, 174–176

ABOUT THE AUTHOR

LLOYD R. SHOEMAKER was born in Salt Lake City, Utah, and enlisted in the U.S. Army in March 1941. Two years later, after being wounded and rotated back to the United States, he was assigned to MIS-X, where he remained until it was disbanded at the end of World War II. Since then, he has been a police officer and a cattle rancher, and has worked for an insurance company. He currently lives in Salem, Oregon.